Day-by-Day Math Thinking Routines in Third Grade

T0372842

Day-by-Day Math Thinking Routines in Third Grade helps you provide students with a review of the foundational ideas in math, every day of the week! Based on the bestselling *Daily Math Thinking Routines in Action*, the book follows the simple premise that frequent, rigorous, engaging practice leads to mastery and retention of concepts, ideas, and skills. These worksheet-free, academically rigorous routines and prompts follow grade level priority standards and include whole group, individual, and partner work. The book can be used with any math program, or for small groups, workstations, or homework.

Inside you will find:

♦ 40 weeks of practice
♦ 1 activity a day
♦ 200 activities total
♦ Answer Key

For each week, the Anchor Routines cover these key areas: Monday: General Thinking Routines; Tuesday: Vocabulary; Wednesday: Place Value; Thursday: Fluency; and Friday: Problem Solving. Get your students' math muscles moving with the easy-to-follow routines in this book!

Dr. Nicki Newton has been an educator for 30 years, working both nationally and internationally with students of all ages. She has worked on developing Math Workshop and Guided Math Institutes around the country; visit her website at www.drnickinewton.com. She is also an avid blogger (www.guidedmath.wordpress.com), tweeter (@drnickimath) and Pinterest pinner (www.pinterest.com/drnicki7).

Day-by-Day Math Thinking Routines in Third Grade

40 Weeks of Quick Prompts and Activities

Dr. Nicki Newton

Routledge
Taylor & Francis Group

NEW YORK AND LONDON

First published 2020
by Routledge
52 Vanderbilt Avenue, New York, NY 10017

and by Routledge
2 Park Square, Milton Park, Abingdon, Oxon, OX14 4RN

Routledge is an imprint of the Taylor & Francis Group, an informa business

Library of Congress Cataloging-in-Publication Data
Names: Newton, Nicki, author.
Title: Day-by-day math thinking routines in third grade : 40 weeks of quick
    prompts and activities / Dr. Nicki Newton.
Description: New York, NY : Routledge, 2020. |
Identifiers: LCCN 2019038953 (print) | LCCN 2019038954 (ebook) |
    ISBN 9780367439170 (hardback) | ISBN 9780367439163 (paperback) |
    ISBN 9781003006442 (ebook)
Subjects: LCSH: Mathematics--Study and teaching (Elementary)--Activity programs.
Classification: LCC QA135.6 .N4848 2020 (print) | LCC QA135.6 (ebook) |
    DDC 372.7/049—dc23
LC record available at https://lccn.loc.gov/2019038953
LC ebook record available at https://lccn.loc.gov/2019038954

ISBN: 978-0-367-43917-0 (hbk)
ISBN: 978-0-367-43916-3 (pbk)
ISBN: 978-1-003-00644-2 (ebk)

Typeset in Palatino
by Swales & Willis, Exeter, Devon, UK

Contents

Meet the Author

Dr. Nicki Newton has been an educator for 30 years, working both nationally and internationally, with students of all ages. Having spent the first part of her career as a literacy and social studies specialist, she built on those frameworks to inform her math work. She believes that math is intricately intertwined with reading, writing, listening, and speaking. She has worked on developing Math Workshop and Guided Math Institutes around the country. Most recently, she has been helping districts and schools nationwide to integrate their State Standards for Mathematics and think deeply about how to teach these within a Math Workshop model. Dr. Nicki works with teachers, coaches, and administrators to make math come alive by considering the powerful impact of building a community of mathematicians who make meaning of real math together. When students do real math, they learn it. They own it, they understand it, and they can do it. Every one of them. Dr. Nicki is also an avid blogger (www.guidedmath. wordpress. com) and Pinterest pinner (https://www.pinterest.com/drnicki7/).

Introduction

Welcome to this exciting new series of daily math thinking routines. I have been doing thinking routines for years. People ask me all the time if I have these written down somewhere. So, I wrote a book. Now, that has turned into a grade level series so that people can do them with prompts that address their grade level standards. This is the anti-worksheet workbook!

The goal is to get students reflecting on their thinking and communicating their mathematical thinking with partners and the whole class about the math they are learning. Marzano (2007)[1] notes that

> initial understanding, albeit a good one, does not suffice for learning that is aimed at long-term retention and use of knowledge. Rather, students must have opportunities to practice new skills and deepen their understanding of new information. Without this type of extended processing, knowledge that students initially understand might fade and be lost over time.

The daily math thinking routines in this book focus on taking Depth of Knowledge (DOK) level 1 activities, to DOK level 2 and 3 activities (Webb, 2005)[2]. Many of the questions are open. For example, we turn the traditional elapsed time question on its head. Instead of asking students "Mark left his house at 3:15 and he came back 20 minutes later. When did he come back?" inspired by Marion Smalls (2009)[3] we ask, "An activity takes 20 minutes. When could it have started and when could it have ended?"

In this series, we mainly work on priority standards, although we do address some of the supporting and additional standards. This book is not intended to cover every standard. Rather, it is meant to provide ongoing daily review of the foundational ideas in math. There is a focus for each day of the week.

- Monday: General Thinking Routines
- Tuesday: Vocabulary
- Wednesday: Place Value
- Thursday: Fluency (American and British Number Talks, Number Strings)
- Friday: Problem Solving

There are general daily thinking routines (What Doesn't Belong?, True or False?, Convince Me!), that review various priority standards from the different domains (Geometry, Algebraic Thinking, Counting, Measurement, Number Sense). Every Tuesday there is an emphasis on Vocabulary because math is a language and if you don't know the words then you can't speak it. There is a continuous review of foundational words through different games (Tic Tac Toe, Match, Vocabulary Bingo), because students need at least 6 encounters with a word to own it. On Wednesday there is often an emphasis on Place Value. Thursday is always some sort of Fluency routine (American or British Number Talks and Number Strings). Finally, Fridays are Problem Solving routines.

1 Marzano, R. J. (2007). *The art and science of teaching: A comprehensive framework for effective instruction.* ASCD: Virginia.
2 Webb, N. (November, 2005). *Depth-of-knowledge levels for four content areas.* Presentation to the Florida Education Research Association, 50th Annual Meeting, Miami, Florida.
3 Small, M. (2009). *Good questions: Great ways to differentiate mathematics instruction.* Teachers College Press: New York.

The book starts with a review of priority and other second grade standards and then as the weeks progress the current grade level standards are integrated throughout. There is a heavy emphasis on work within 10 and place value within 120. There is also an emphasis on geometry concepts and some data and measurement. The word problem types for third grade have been woven throughout the year.

Throughout the book there is an emphasis on the mathematical practices/processes (SMP, 2010[4]; NCTM, 2000[5]). Students are expected to problem solve in different ways. They are expected to reason by contextualizing and decontextualizing numbers. They are expected to communicate their thinking to partners and the whole group using the precise mathematical vocabulary. Part of this is reading the work of others, listening to others' explanations, writing about their work, and then speaking about their work and the work of others in respectful ways. Students are expected to model their thinking with tools and templates. Students are continuously asked to think about the pattern and structure of numbers as they work through the activities.

These activities focus on building mathematical proficiency as defined by the NAP 2001[6]. These activities focus on conceptual understanding, procedural fluency, adaptive reasoning, strategic competence and a student's mathematical disposition. This book can be used with any math program. These are jump starters to the day. They will get the math muscle moving at the beginning of the day.

Math routines are a form of "guided practice." Marzano notes that although the

guided practice is the place where students—working alone, with other students, or with the teacher—engage in the cognitive processing activities of organizing, reviewing, rehearsing, summarizing, comparing, and contrasting. However, it is important that all students engage in these activities. (p. 7)

These are engaging, standards-based, academically rigorous activities that provide meaningful routines that develop mathematical proficiency. The work can also be used for practice within small groups, workstations and also sent home home as questions for homework.

We have focused on coherence from grade to grade, rigor of thinking, and focus on understanding and being able to explain the math the students are doing. We have intended to take deeper dives into the math, not rushing to the topics of the next grade but going deeper into the topics of the grade at hand. Here is our criteria for selecting the routines:

♦ Engaging
♦ Easy to learn
♦ Repeatable
♦ Open-ended
♦ Easy to differentiate (adapt and extend for different levels).

4 The Standards of Mathematical Practice. "Common Core State Standards for Mathematical Practice." Washington, D.C.: National Governors Association Center for Best Practices, Council of Chief State School Officers, 2010. Retrieved on December 1, 2019 from: www.corestandards.org/Math/Practice.
5 National Council of Teachers of Mathematics. (2000). *Principles and standards for school mathematics.* Reston, VA: National Council of Teachers of Mathematics.
6 Kilpatrick, J., Swafford, J., and Findell, B. (eds.) (2001). *Adding it up: Helping children learn mathematics.* Washington, DC: National Academy Press.

Figure 1.1 Talking About the Routine!

Monday: Reasoning about Numbers

3 + ___ = 7

Jen said that the answer is 10. Kelly said the answer is 4. Who do you agree with? Why?

Tuesday: Vocabulary Bingo

Look at the 4 words. Decide which one doesn't belong and why. Discuss with a partner.

difference	subtract
addend	take away

Wednesday: Guess My Number

Read the riddle. Think about the clues. Discuss what you think the answer is with a classmate.

I am a 2-digit number.
I am more than 12.
I am less than 20.
My digits add up to 9.
What number am I?

Thursday: Number Strings

7 + 4
7 + 5
7 + 6
7 + 7

Friday: Word Problem Fill-in

Mike had _____ marbles. He gave _____ away. How many did he have left?
    (4 or 5)   (1, 2, or 3)

Figure 1.2 The Math Routine Cycle of Engagement

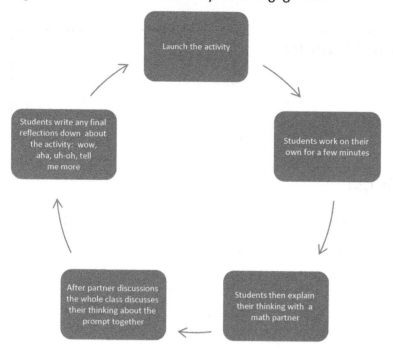

Step 1: Students are given the launch prompt. The teacher explains the prompt and makes sure that everyone understands what they are working on.

Step 2: They are given a few minutes to work on that prompt by themselves.

Step 3: The next step is for students to work with a math partner. As they work with this partner, students are expected to listen to what their partner did as well as explain their own work.

Step 4: Students come back together as a whole group and discuss the math. They are encouraged to talk about how they solved it and the similarities and differences between their thinking and their partner's thinking.

Step 5: Students reflect on the prompt of the day, thinking about what wowed them, what made them say "Aha," what made them say "Uh-oh," what made them say, "I need to know more about this."

Thinking Activities

These are carefully planned practice activities to get students to think. They are **not meant to be used as a workbook**. This is a thinking activity book. The emphasis is on students doing their own work, explaining what they did with a partner and then sharing out to the entire class.

Overview of the Routines

Monday Routines – General Thinking Routines (Algebraic Thinking, Measurement, Data, Geometry)

- 2 Arguments
- 3 Truths and a Fib
- Alike and Different
- Always, Sometimes, Never
- Break It up!
- Convince Me!
- Input/Output Table
- It Is/It Isn't
- Legs and Feet
- Magic Squares
- Missing Number
- Number Line It!
- Pattern That!
- Reasoning About Numbers
- Reasoning Matrices
- Tic Tac Toe
- Elapsed Time
- True or False?
- What Doesn't Belong?
- Why Is It Not?
- Venn Diagram

Tuesday Routines – Vocabulary

- 1-Minute Essay/Quick Write
- Frayer Model
- It Is/It isn't
- Vocabulary Bingo
- Vocabulary Brainstorm
- Vocabulary Fill-in
- Vocabulary Match
- Vocabulary 1-Minute Essay/Quick Write
- Vocabulary Reflection
- Vocabulary Tic Tac Toe
- What Doesn't Belong?

Wednesday Routines – Place Value

- 3 Truths and a Fib
- Convince Me!
- Find and Fix the Error
- Fraction of the Day
- Greater Than, Less Than, in Between
- Guess My Number
- How Many More to

- Money Mix
- Number Bond It!
- Number Line It!
- Number of the Day
- Patterns/Skip Counting
- Round That!
- True or False?
- What Doesn't Belong?
- What's Missing?
- Venn Diagram

Thursday Routines – Number Talk

- British Number Talk
- Find and Fix the Error
- Number Strings
- Number Talk

Friday Routines – Problem Solving

- Equation Match
- Make Your Own Problem
- Model That!
- Pattern That!
- Picture That!
- Sort That!
- What's the Question? (3 Read Protocol)
- What's the Story?
- Word Problem Fill-in
- Word Problem Sort
- Write a Problem

Figure 1.3 Overview of the Routines

Routine	Purpose	Description
1-Minute Essay/Quick Write	In this routine, students have to think about, discuss, and write about a concept.	Students write about a topic, their friend adds information, and then they write some more about the topic.
2 Arguments	In this reasoning routine, students are thinking about common errors that students make when doing various math tasks like missing numbers, working with properties, and working with the equal sign.	Students listen to the way 2 different students approached a problem, decide who they agree with, and defend their thinking.
3 Truths and a Fib	In this routine, students have to consider whether or not statements are true or false.	Students are given 3 statements that are true and 1 statement that is false. They have to choose the false one and discuss their thinking.
Alike and Different	This routine focuses on students reasoning about how 2 things are alike and different.	Students are given 2 figures or words and they have to discuss how they are alike and how they are different.
Always, Sometimes, Never	This routine focuses on students reasoning about whether a statement is always, sometimes, or never true.	In this routine, students are given a statement and they have to argue and prove their thinking about if the statement is always, sometimes, or never true.
Break It up!	In this routine, students work on the distributive property.	In this routine, students are given an expression and they have to sketch it and then break it apart using the distributive property.
Convince Me!	This routine focuses on students reasoning about different topics. They have to convince their peers about specific statements.	Students are given different things to think about like statements or equations and they have to convince their peers that they are correct.
Elapsed Time	This routine is an open question, where students work with elapsed time.	Students have to write an elapsed time problem.
Equation Match	This routine focuses on students thinking about which operation they would use to solve a problem. It requires that they reason about the actions that are happening in the problem and then what they are required to do to solve the problem.	Students have to match the word problem and the equation.

Routine	Purpose	Description
Find and Fix the Error	This routine requires that students analyze the work of others and discuss what went well or what went wrong. The purpose of the routine is not only to get students to identify common errors but also to get them to justify their own thinking about the problem.	Students think about a problem either by themselves, with a partner, or with the whole group that is either done correctly or incorrectly. They have to figure out why it has been done incorrectly or correctly and discuss.
Fraction of the Day	This routine focuses on students thinking about and modeling fractions.	Students are given a fraction and they have to write it in word form, draw a visual model, plot it on a number line, and discuss it in relationship to other fractions.
Frayer Model	This routine is meant to get students talking about concepts. They are supposed to talk about the definition, what happens in real life, sketch an example, and also give non-examples.	Students are given a template with labels. They work through the template writing and drawing about the specified topic.
Guess My Number	This routine gives students a variety of clues about a number and asks the students to guess which number it might be, given all the clues. Students have to use their understanding of place value and math vocabulary to figure out which number is being discussed.	Students are given various clues about a number and they must use the clues to guess which number it is.
Greater Than, Less Than, in Between	In this routine, students talk about numbers specifically in terms of being greater than, less than, or in between each other.	Students are thinking about the number relationships and filling in boxes based on those relationships.
How Many More to	In this routine, students are asked to tell how many to a specific number. Again, this is another place value routine, asking students to reason about numbers on the number line.	Students are given a specific number and they have to tell how many more to get to the target number.
Input/Output Table	This routine focuses on getting students to think about patterns.	Students have to fill in the number of the Input/Output Table and in some cases create their own from scratch.
It Is/It Isn't	This routine can be used in a variety of ways. Students have to look at the topic and decide what it is and what it isn't. It is another way of looking at the idea of example and non-example.	Students discuss what something is and what it isn't.

Routine	Purpose	Description
Legs and Feet	Legs and Feet is a great arithmetic routine which gets students to use various operations to figure out how many animals there are by working with numbers.	Students look at different animals and think about how many legs and feet there could be, given that number of animals.
Magic Squares	In this fluency routine, students are working with math puzzles to figure out missing numbers.	There are a few different ways to do Magic Squares. One way is for students to figure out what the magic number is by calculating to find it in all directions.
Make Your Own Problem	In this word problem routine students get to pick their own numbers to create and then solve a word problem.	Students fill in the blanks with numbers to make their own problems.
Model That!	In this word problem routine, students are focusing on representing word problems in a variety of ways.	Students have to represent their thinking about a word problem with various models.
Missing Number	This routine focuses on students' thinking about missing numbers.	Many of the Missing Number activities require that students reason about what number it should be.
Money Mix	This routine focuses on students' knowledge of money.	The money routines have students counting and comparing money quantities.
Number Bond It!	In this routine, students are working on decomposing numbers in a variety of ways.	Students use number bonds to break apart numbers in different ways.
Number of the Day	This activity focuses on students modeling numbers in a variety of ways.	This activity has a given number and students have to represent that number in different ways.
Number Line It!	This activity focuses on students sequencing numbers correctly.	Students have to put numbers in the correct sequence on the number line.
British Number Talk	This routine focuses on students thinking about their thinking.	Students have to choose their own problems and discuss how they are going to solve them. They must name the way they did it, either in their head, with a model, or with an algorithm.

Routine	Purpose	Description
Number Talk	This activity focuses on number sense. Students compose and decompose numbers as well as add and subtract numbers.	There are a few different ways that students do this activity. One approach involves the teacher working with the students on showing a number in a variety of ways. Another activity is that the teacher gives the students number strings around a specific concept (for example, subtracting 1 from a number) and students work those problems and discuss the strategy.
Number Strings	In this routine, students are looking at the relationship between a set of problems.	Students work out the different problems and think and discuss the various strategies they are using.
Patterns/Skip Counting	In this routine, students focus on patterns.	Many of the pattern activities require students to fill in a pattern and then make their own patterns.
Picture That!	In this routine, students discuss a picture.	Many of these activities require that students look at a picture and make up a math word problem about the picture.
Reasoning about Numbers	In this routine, students reason about adding and subtracting numbers.	Students are asked to reason about numbers.
Reasoning Matrices	In these routines, students have to reason about math topics.	Students are asked to reason about people given specific facts.
Round That!	In this routine, students work on rounding.	The rounding activities ask students to come up with the numbers that can be rounded rather than giving students a number to round.
Sort That!	In this routine, students work on sorting word problem types.	Students have to figure out the types of problems they are solving.
True or False?	This activity focuses on students reasoning about what is true or false.	Students are given different things to think about like statements about shapes or equations and they have to state and prove whether they are true or false.
Venn Diagram	In this routine, students create a Venn diagram with specific criteria.	Students are given a Venn diagram that they must fill out based on specific criteria.

Routine	Purpose	Description
Vocabulary Bingo	This is the traditional bingo game with a focus on vocabulary.	Students play Vocabulary Bingo but they have to discuss the vocabulary and make drawings or write definitions to show they know what the word means. Teachers will need to make copies of the boards for students. Or the students can play it in teams as a class on the board.
Vocabulary Brainstorm	In this routine, students have to brainstorm about vocabulary words.	Students have to write about different vocabulary words.
Vocabulary Match	In this routine, the focus is on working with the math vocabulary from across the year.	Students match the vocabulary with the definition.
Vocabulary Fill-in	In this routine students work on vocabulary.	Students are given sentences with missing vocabulary words that they must fill in the correct spaces.
Vocabulary Reflection	In this routine students reflect on the vocabulary they have learned this year.	In this routine, students discuss vocabulary that they have learned.
Vocabulary Tic Tac Toe	In this routine, students are working on math vocabulary words from across the year.	Students play Vocabulary Tic Tac Toe by taking turns to choose a square and then sketch or write on the side to illustrate the word. Whoever gets 3 in a row first wins. Teachers will need to make copies of the boards for students. Or the students can play it in teams as a class on the board.
Why Is It Not?	This routine focuses on students looking at error patterns and correcting them.	Students have to look at error patterns and then discuss what the correct answer should be and prove why.
What Doesn't Belong?	This is a reasoning activity where students have to choose which objects they can group together and why. The emphasis is on justification.	Students have 4 squares. They have to figure out which object does not belong.
What's the Question? (3 Read Protocol)	The purpose is for students to slow down and consider all of the parts of the word problem.	Students have to read the problem 3 times. The first time they focus on the context. The second time they focus on the numbers. The third time they focus on asking questions that would make sense given the context.

Routine	Purpose	Description
What's the Story?	This routine focuses on students making sense of numbers.	Students have to look at the model and make up a story that matches it.
Word Problem Sort	In this routine, students are reason about what type of problem they are looking at.	Students sort the problems and decide which one is the designated type that they are looking for.
Word Problem Fill-in	In this routine, students have to fill in numbers and make up and solve their own word problem.	Students fill in the blanks with numbers that they choose and then model and solve the word problem.
Write a Problem	In this routine, students have to write their own problems.	Students have to write problems based on an equation or based on a topic.

Questioning Is the Key

Unlock the Magic of Thinking, You Need Good Questions!

Figure 1.4

Launch Questions (Before the Activity)	Process Questions (During the Activity)
♦ What is this prompt asking us to do? ♦ How will you start? ♦ What are you thinking? ♦ Explain to your math partner, your understanding of the question. ♦ What will you do to solve this problem?	♦ What will you do first? ♦ How will you organize your thinking? ♦ What might you do to get started? ♦ What is your strategy? ♦ Why did you … ? ♦ Why are you doing that? ♦ Is that working? Does it make sense? ♦ Is that a reasonable answer? ♦ Can you prove it? ♦ Are you sure about that answer? ♦ How do you know you are correct?
Debrief Questions (After the Activity) ♦ What did you do? ♦ How did you get your answer? ♦ How do you know it is correct? ♦ Can you prove it? ♦ Convince me that you have the correct answer. ♦ Is there another way to think about this problem?	**Partner Questions (Guide Student Conversations)** ♦ Tell me what you did. ♦ Tell me more about your model. ♦ Tell me more about your drawing. ♦ Tell me more about your calculations. ♦ Tell me more about your thinking. ♦ Can you prove it? ♦ How do you know you are right? ♦ I understand what you did. ♦ I don't understand what you did yet.

Daily Routines

Monday: What Doesn't Belong?

When doing What Doesn't Belong?, have the students do the calculations (in their journals, on scratch paper, or on the activity page). Then, have them share their thinking with a friend. Finally, pull them back to the group.

Often students will pick the most obvious difference. For example, they might say 20 – 12 doesn't belong because it is a subtraction problem. This is true. I would ask them what the difference is between addition and subtraction. I would ask if there are other ways we can think about this first set of numbers. You want someone to say that 6 + 4 + 3 doesn't belong because the sum is 13.

So, in this routine it is important to also focus on language for the descriptions. The language should be something like: 6 + 4 + 3 doesn't belong because its sum is 13 and all the other problems have a sum or difference of 12. In Set B, most of the problems are subtraction. Some students will say it's the addition problem. Accept that answer and then look for others. Always validate and affirm what students say. Work it into an ongoing conversation. For example: "Yes that is true. What else might we think about this set?" You want students to be able to say "The difference or the sum to all the other expressions is 15 but for 50 – 25 the difference is 25. So, the expression 50 – 25 doesn't belong!"

Tuesday: Vocabulary Match

This Vocabulary Match has many of the second grade words that students should know. Often when reviewing vocabulary it is good to review the grade level words mixed up, meaning not by a specific category. Students should say the word and then find the matching definition. They should have some minutes to do this on their own and then an opportunity to go over their thinking with their math partner. Then, after about 5 minutes, bring them back together as a group and discuss the thinking. Ask students which words were tricky and which ones were easy. Also ask them if there were any that they didn't recognize, that they have never seen before. Have them draw a little sketch by each word to help them remember the word.

Wednesday: Convince Me!

This routine is about getting students to defend and justify their thinking. Be sure to emphasize the language of reasoning. Students should focus on proving it with numbers, words, and pictures. They should say things like:

This is true! I can prove it with ...

This is the difference because ...

I am going to use _____ to show my thinking.

I am going to defend my answer by _____.

I proved my thinking using addition.

*Note: this is the perfect opportunity for students to relate the operations. We always want them thinking about the relationship between the operations.

There are a few tools for students to use but they are in no way limited to those tools.

Thursday: Number Talk

In this Number Talk you want the students to discuss their thinking with strategies and models. Ask students about the strategies that they might use.

Possible responses:

Break apart the tens and the ones and add them.

Give and Take (Compensation) – Take 1 from 28 and give it to 29 to make 30 and 28 becomes 27. Discuss how this makes it a much easier problem when we work with tens.

Friday: What's the Question?

The focus of today is to do a 3 read problem with the students. It is important to read the problem 3 times out loud as a choral read with the students.

First Read: (Stop and visualize! What do you see?) What is this story about? Who is in it? What are they doing?

Second Read: What are the numbers? What do they mean?

Third Read: What are some possible questions we could ask about this story?

Possible questions:

How many marbles does Mary have altogether?

How many fewer red marbles does she have than blue ones?

How many more blue marbles does she have than pink ones?

Does she have more than 20 marbles in total?

How many more pink ones does she need in order to have the same amount of pink as she does red?

How many red and blue marbles does she have in total?

What is the sum of the blue and pink marbles?

*Note: Focus on the vocabulary. Use different words for the sum (altogether, total).

Focus on different types of comparative language so students get comfortable with words and phrases like: "how many more," "how many less," "how many more to get the same amount as," "how many fewer"?

Week 1 Activities

Monday: What Doesn't Belong?

Choose the item that doesn't belong in each set.

A.

7 + 5	20 – 8
6 + 4 + 3	4 + 4 + 4

B.

20 – 5	30 – 15
5 + 5 + 5	50 – 25

Tuesday: Vocabulary Match

Match the words with the correct definitions.

sum   a 6-sided figure

addend   the answer to an addition problem

centimeter   one of the numbers in an addition equation

difference   the answer to a subtraction problem

hexagon   a small unit of measure

Wednesday: Convince Me!

Prove it with numbers, words, and/or pictures!

$87 - 25 = 62$

1	2	3	4	5	6	7	8	9	10
11	12	13	14	15	16	17	18	19	20
21	22	23	24	25	26	27	28	29	30
31	32	33	34	35	36	37	38	39	40
41	42	43	44	45	46	47	48	49	50
51	52	53	54	55	56	57	58	59	60
61	62	63	64	65	66	67	68	69	70
71	72	73	74	75	76	77	78	79	80
81	82	83	84	85	86	87	88	89	90
91	92	93	94	95	96	97	98	99	100

Thursday: Number Talk

What are some ways to think about:

$$29 + 28$$

Friday: What's the Question?

Think of at least 2 questions you could ask about this story. Write them down. Discuss with your classmates.

Mary has 12 red marbles, 14 blue marbles, and 6 pink ones.

1)

2)

Week 2 Teacher Notes

Monday: Magic Squares

Magic Squares are great for practice. They are intriguing, fun, and fast paced. Students want to get the answer and they get right to work. In this first Magic Square students are trying to figure out the target number (the one that the digits add up to no matter which way you calculate them – horizontally, vertically, or diagonally. Have the students work on it on their own, then share their thinking with a partner. Then, bring everyone back to the whole group and have them discuss it. In the next Magic Square students have to make 15 in all directions by filling in the missing numbers.

Tuesday: Vocabulary Tic Tac Toe

These are quick partner energizers. Read all the words together. Then go! The students have 7 minutes to play the game. They play rock, paper, scissors to see who starts. They then take turns choosing words and explaining it to their partner. Then, they have to do a sketch or something to show they understand the word. Everybody should play the first game, if they have time, they can play the next one.

* Note: It is important to call everyone back together at the end and talk about the vocabulary. Briefly go over the vocabulary, this is all second grade vocabulary.

Wednesday: Number Line It!

In this Number Line It! routine the students are working with numbers 0 to 500. This is actually a much more difficult skill than it seems. Students often have trouble thinking about how to place the numbers on the number line. There should be an emphasis on doing this absolutely accurately. So, students should be encouraged to think about where the numbers might go, put a tick on the line, discuss it with their partner, defend their thinking, and then to go back and put the numbers on the line. After students have placed their numbers on the line, the whole class comes back together and discusses what has been done. The more that students do this, the better they get.

Thursday: Number Talk

There are a variety of numbers in the circles so that students can choose a variety of problems. Encourage them to take risks. Talk about maybe picking some easy problems and then some tricky ones.

Friday: Sort That!

In this routine, students have to read and think about the problems. They have to reason and decide which one of these is a taking from situation. One way to approach this is to read each problem out loud and then have students discuss that particular problem with their math partner. Do this for each of the 4 problems and then have the students discuss which one they think it is. They should defend their thinking to their partner and then the whole class comes back together and discusses their thinking.

Week 2 Activities

Monday: Magic Squares

What is the Magic Number? It should be the same adding horizontally, diagonally, and vertically.

4	9	2
3	5	7
8	1	6

Make 15 by adding numbers that make 15 going in all directions.

2		4
	5	

Tuesday: Vocabulary Tic Tac Toe

Do rock, paper, scissors to decide who goes first. Pick a square. Write a description or draw a picture of the answer on the side. Then, put an x or o. If your partner disagrees, look it up. If the player is correct, they go again. If wrong, they lose the turn.

Game 1: Explain these words			Game 2: Say the name of the shape
sum	addend	subtract	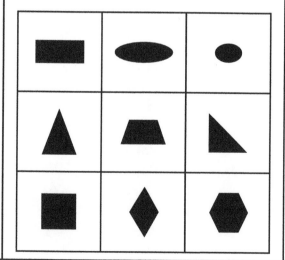
inch	centimeter	difference	
total	altogether	add	

Wednesday: Number Line It!

Place these numbers on the number line in the correct order, as accurately as possible.

182   230   350   99   50   475

⟵───⟶

0   500

Compare these with your partner. Explain your thinking. How do you know you are correct?

Thursday: Number Talk

Pick a number from each circle. Then, decide how you are going to solve it. Write the problem under the way you solved it. For example: 8 + 2. I can do that in my head because it is a ten friend.

Did I do it in my head?	Did I use a model?	Did I write down the numbers and solve it on paper?

8   17   9
5   6   7   1
1   2   0
9   10   50

8   9   5
6   7
1   2   0   15
19   10   50
25   19

Friday: Sort That!

Put a line under the take away problems. Put a circle around the join problems. Answer all the problems.

Justify your thinking with a partner and then share with the whole group.

A. Sue had 15 marbles. She got 15 more. How many does she have now?

B. Luke had 100 marbles. He gave 15 away. How many does he have now?

C. Marco had 27 marbles. His brother gave him 12 more. How many does he have now?

D. Maria had 18 marbles. She got some more. Now she has 27 How many did she get?

Week 3 Teacher Notes

Monday: Always, Sometimes, Never

In this routine you are trying to get students to reason. So they should try out what they think by writing down at least 3 examples and discussing them with their partner. After they have discussed their thinking with their partner, the class should come back together and discuss their thinking. The emphasis should be on proving whatever they believe.

Tuesday: Vocabulary Bingo

Today the focus of the vocabulary is on fractions and time. Students have worked with all of these words in prior grades. Remember that you are trying to normalize these words in the students' vocabulary. They should be comfortable with the fractions that they have already studied; halves, thirds, and fourths. You want students to also understand this idea of the whole. Other words in this bingo game are the operation words (including decompose) because we need students to understand these words and be using them when they are working on multi-digit addition and subtraction strategies. Also, later on, when they start working with multiplication problems, they will use these words to work with the distributive property. Then, there are the words polygon and half past. Again, the idea is to keep math vocabulary up and present in the minds of students. As the teacher calls the words, use illustrations, definitions and the words.

Wednesday: Number of the Day

Number of the Day is important and reviews place value skills. There are both closed and open items in the routine. Give the students about 5 minutes to work on this and discuss it with their math partner. Then, come back together as a class and talk about what the students did.

Thursday: Number Strings

Students should discuss the strings as a whole class. You want the emphasis to be on the relationships between the numbers. Students should be thinking about whether they know one of the base facts and how it helps them with the other facts. Sometimes, people call these "helper" facts. Although these are first and second grade strategies, many third graders are still very shaky with these, thus the ongoing review.

Friday: Model That!

The focus for this Friday is the open number line. This was a second grade model. We want students to be very comfortable with the open number line. Encourage them to use it often, along with the tape diagram. Focus on the idea of jumping tens and multiples of tens. They can do this in a variety of ways. They could add up all the tens and then the ones. They could also start at a number and then jump to the nearest tens from there. For example, 89 + 1 would get you to 90 and then add 50 and then from 140 add 60 to get to 200 and add 6 more. Also, students could just add 50, 60, and 80 to get 190 and then add 16 more. Another way to do it is to first adjust 89 to 90 by taking one from 67 and then add 50, 60, and 90 to get 200 and then add 6 more.

Week 3 Activities

Monday: Always, Sometimes, Never

Read the statement and decide if it is always, sometimes, or never true. Justify your thinking with numbers, words, and/or pictures.

If you add 3 numbers the answer will always be odd.

Tuesday: Vocabulary Bingo

Put each of the words in a box in a different order than they appear. Play bingo. When the teacher calls a word, cover it. Whoever gets 4 in a row vertically, horizontally, or diagonally or any 4 corners wins.

Words: fourths, thirds, halves, denominator, numerator, whole, sum, difference, addend, decompose, polygon, quarter past, half past, noon, hexagon, octagon.

Write a word in each space.

Wednesday: Number of the Day

Fill in the boxes.

99

Number word form	Show 2 addition sentences that make 99.
Show 2 subtraction sentences that make 99	Add 3 numbers that make 99

Thursday: Number Strings

Discuss the numbers. What do you notice?

String 1	String 2
7 + 7	7 + 5
7 + 6	17 + 5
7 + 5	17 + 6
7 + 4	17 + 7
	17 + 8

Friday: Model That!

Sue jumped 35 cm, 67 cm and then 18 cm. How far did she jump in total?

Model on the open number line.

A.

1	2	3	4	5	6	7	8	9	10
11	12	13	14	15	16	17	18	19	20
21	22	23	24	25	26	27	28	29	30
31	32	33	34	35	36	37	38	39	40
41	42	43	44	45	46	47	48	49	50
51	52	53	54	55	56	57	58	59	60
61	62	63	64	65	66	67	68	69	70
71	72	73	74	75	76	77	78	79	80
81	82	83	84	85	86	87	88	89	90
91	92	93	94	95	96	97	98	99	100
101	102	103	104	105	106	107	108	109	110
111	112	113	114	115	116	117	118	119	120

B. Break it apart.

Monday: Magic Square

In this Magic Square students have to fill in the missing numbers. Remember that Magic Squares are made to foster flexibility. Give the students a few minutes to work on it by themselves and then have them discuss their thinking with their math partner. Then, come back together as a class and have the students discuss their thinking.

Tuesday: It Is/It Isn't

In this routine you want students to be focusing on the vocabulary. Encourage students to use the word bank. This is a scaffold only though. This is to get them started. The conversation might sound something like this: "It is a 2-digit number. It is not a 1-digit number. It is an odd number. It is not an even number. It is greater than 20. It is less than 90. It is in between 30 and 60. It is 10 more than 43. It is 10 less than 63."

Wednesday: Greater Than, Less Than, in Between

In this routine, students are thinking about the number relationships. Have the students do it on their own and then talk with their math partners. Then, bring them back together as a class and discuss it.

Thursday: Number Talk

This is a typical Number Talk where students are thinking about the ways in which they can solve this subtraction problem. You want students to think about partial differences, counting up, and compensation. For example:

I add 1 to each number. I changed the problem to 75 and 30. That made it easy. I subtracted 30 from 75 and that is 45.

Another student might say:

I started at 29 and jumped 1 to 30 and then 44 more to 74. I added 1 and 44 and I got 45 as the difference.

Another student might say:

I took away 20 from 74 and I got 54. Then, I took away another 10 and I got 44 but I added 1 back because I took to many away and I got 45.

Friday: Picture That!

Students look at the box of donuts and write any type of story they want to. They can work on this with their partner. Then they should be ready to share it out with the whole class.

Week 4 Activities

Monday: Magic Square

The magic number is 15. Fill in the spaces so that they make 15 by adding them in any direction.

8		6
	5	

Tuesday: It Is/It Isn't

Describe what the word is and isn't.

53

It Is	It Isn't

Wednesday: Greater Than, Less Than, in Between

150   325   990

Name a number greater than 150	Name a number in between 325 and 990	Name a number greater than the difference of 325 and 150
Name a number greater than the sum of 150 and 325	Name a number in between 150 and 325	Name a number less than the difference between 990 and 150

Thursday: Number Talk

What are some ways to solve 74 − 29?

Friday: Picture That!

Tell a story about this box of donuts.

Story:

Equation:

Monday: 2 Arguments

Students look at this problem and discuss it with their math partner. The emphasis should be on proving their thinking. They should discuss how what they have said is true. Then, everyone should come back together and discuss it.

Tuesday: Vocabulary Match

Say all the words together as a class and get students to think about if they know these words, if they are familiar, or if they are completely unfamiliar. Then, have students turn and work with their partners on the match. Come back together as a class and discuss the words.

Wednesday: Money Mix

Money is challenging for many students. They worked on it a great deal in second grade, so this is a way of reviewing that content and building flexibility with numbers. Students should do it on their own, then share their thinking with a partner, and finally come back together and discuss it with the class.

Thursday: Number Talk

Give students about 5 minutes to work on their own or with partners to come up with some problems, hopefully from each category so that they stretch themselves. You don't want them to only choose easy problems. Then, students should share what they did with the class.

Friday: Make Your Own Problem

Give students about 5 minutes to do their own fill-in problems and share them with their math partner. Their partner has to tell them if their problem makes sense. Then, some students will share their thinking with the class.

Week 5 Activities

Monday: 2 Arguments

Read both arguments. Decide who you agree with and explain your thinking.

$8 + \_\_\_\_ = 50$

John said the answer was 58.

Maria said the answer was 42.

Who do you agree with? Why?

Tuesday: Vocabulary Match

Match the words with the definitions.

hundreds

hexagon

thousands $100 + 30 + 5$

expanded   4,091
form

trapezoid   160

Wednesday: Money Mix

Raul had 50 cents. Show 3 different combinations of coins he could have had.

Way 1	Way 2	Way 3

Thursday: Number Talk

Pick a number from each circle. Then, decide how you are going to solve it. Write the problem under the way you solved it. For example, 8 + 2. I can do that in my head because it is a ten friend.

Did I do it in my head?	Did I use a model?	Did I write down the numbers and solve it on paper?

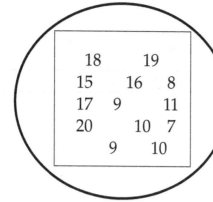

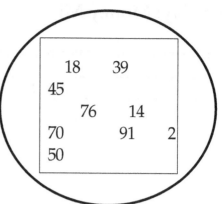

Friday: Make Your Own Problem

Use 2-digit numbers. Fill in the blanks and then solve the problem.

Ray had _____ marbles. He got _____ more for his birthday. How many marbles does he have now?

Model it!

Number sentence (equation): _____

Monday: It Is/It Isn't

In this routine you want students to be focusing on the vocabulary. Encourage students to use the word bank. This is a scaffold only though. This is to get them started. The conversation might sound something like this: "It is a polygon. It is not a quadrilateral. It has 6 sides. It does not have curved sides."

Tuesday: 1-Minute Essay/Quick Write

Give students the designated part of the time to write everything they can about polygons and then share and then write again and finally share out with the class.

Wednesday: Find and Fix the Error

Students have to look at the problem with their math partner and discuss what is incorrect. Then, figure out how they would fix it. They should be ready to come back and discuss it with the class.

Thursday: Number Strings

Students should discuss the string as a whole class. You want the emphasis to be on the relationships between the numbers. In this string we are working on what happens with 9s. Students should recognize that we can just compensate and make the 9 into a 10 and add from there. With practice, students do this naturally.

Friday: Equation Match

Getting students to match the story to the equation is so important because this is often where students struggle. This activity gets them to slow down and think about what the numbers actually represent in the problem. Let students work on this with their math partner and then be ready to share this with the entire class.

Monday: It Is/It Isn't

Describe what the word is and isn't.

Hexagon

It Is	It Isn't

Tuesday: 1-Minute Essay/Quick Write

(For 30 seconds) Write everything you can about polygons. Use numbers, words, and pictures.

(15 seconds) Now switch with a neighbor and add 1 thing to their list.

(15 seconds) Now add 1 more thing to your list.

Wednesday: Find and Fix the Error

Read the problem. Decide what was done wrong and fix it.

John did this. The answer is wrong. Find and fix the error.

$$\begin{array}{r} 100 \\ -\ 59 \\ \hline 159 \end{array}$$

1. What is wrong?

2. Why can't you do what John did?

3. Fix it.

4. Explain your thinking to your partner and then the whole group.

Thursday: Number Strings

$$29 + 4$$
$$19 + 24$$
$$29 + 64$$
$$59 + 74$$

Friday: Equation Match

Which equation matches the story and why?

Jan had some marbles. She got 71 more. Now she has 100. How many did she have in the beginning?

A. $71 + ? = ?$
B. $? + 71 = 100$
C. $100 + 71 = ?$
D. Equation is not here.

Monday: 3 Truths and a Fib

This is a measurement reasoning activity. In second grade, these were priority topics. This is about that ongoing review.

Tuesday: Vocabulary Brainstorm

Students have to think and then write about the word in all of the thought clouds. They first share their thinking with a partner and then share it with the whole class.

Wednesday: Patterns/Skip Counting

Students fill in the pattern, discuss their thinking with a neighbor and then discuss as a whole class. It is really important that students make their own pattern as well. Time must be given to students to do this.

Thursday: Number Talk

In this Number Talk you want students to either count up or think about adjusting the numbers to make the problem easier. If students subtracted 2 from each number, the problem would stay the same but be easier to calculate. So the new problem would become 89 – 52. Students should be shown how they are just shifting the number line and that the difference is staying the same.

Friday: Equation Match

Getting students to match the story to the equation is so important because this is often where students struggle. In this particular example, they are given the equation and then just 2 problems to pick from. This activity gets them to slow down and think about what the numbers actually represent in the problem. Let students work on this with their math partner and then be ready to share this with the entire class.

Monday: 3 Truths and a Fib

Read the statements. Which one is false? Why? Explain to your neighbor and then the group.

A baseball bat is about 40 yards.
An ant is about a centimeter long.
A door is about 8 feet.
A bee is about an inch long.

Tuesday: Vocabulary Brainstorm

Subtraction – In each thought cloud write or draw something that has to do with subtraction.

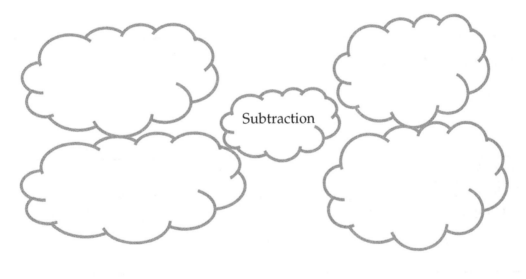

Subtraction

Wednesday: Patterns/Skip Counting

Complete and describe the following patterns:

1. 106, 104, _____, _____, _____, 96

2. 55, ___, 59, ____, 63, 65, 67, ____, ____

3. Make your own:

   ____, ____, ____, ____, ____, ____, ____, ____

Thursday: Number Talk

What are some ways to solve 91 – 54?

Friday: Equation Match

What's the problem? Why?

$$100 - m = 77$$

Problem A	Problem B
Kelly had 100 marbles. She got 77 more. How many does she have now?	Kelly had 100 marbles. She gave some away and now she has 77. How many did she give away?

Monday: True or False?

Many times, students are quick to dismiss this as not being a hexagon, because it is unfamiliar as a hexagon. So, have students think about it and debate it with a partner before discussing it with the whole class. It is really important to follow up by having the students draw another hexagon. Encourage them to draw an irregular hexagon (one that does not have all equal sides).

Tuesday: Vocabulary Tic Tac Toe

These are quick partner energizers. Read all the words together. Then go! The students have 7 minutes to play the game. They play rock, paper, scissors to see who starts. They then take turns choosing words and explaining it to their partner. Then, they have to do a sketch or something to show they understand the word. Everybody should play the first game, if they have time, they can play the next one.

* Note: It is important to call everyone back together at the end and talk about the vocabulary. Briefly go over the vocabulary, this is all second grade vocabulary.

Wednesday: Number Bond It!

Number bonds are important because they build flexibility. Students should be thinking about how to compose and decompose numbers in a variety of ways. Have the students work on this by themselves first and then discuss with a partner, and finally with the entire class.

Thursday: Number Talk

Give students about 5 minutes to work on their own or with partners to come up with some subtraction problems, hopefully from each category so that they stretch themselves. You don't want them to only choose the easy problem. Then, students should share what they did with the class.

Friday: Model That!

The focus here is that students use the tape diagram. Although we want students to use a variety of models, they have to learn them first so that they have a repertoire to choose from. They started working on tape diagrams in second grade, so it good to work on these every chance you get.

Week 8 Activities

Monday: True or False?

This is a hexagon.

1. Think about it.
2. Share your thinking with a partner. Defend your answer.
3. Share your thinking with the group.
4. Draw another type of hexagon.

Tuesday: Vocabulary Tic Tac Toe

Do rock, paper, scissors to decide who goes first. Pick a square. Write a description or draw a picture of the answer on the side. Then, put an x or o. If your partner disagrees, look it up. If the player is correct, they go again. If wrong, they lose the turn.

A.

addend	centimeter	hundreds
equal	thousands	digit
equation	octagon	expanded form

B.

fewer	greater	yard
feet	inch	compare
expanded form	pentagon	cylinder

Wednesday: Number Bond It!

Show how to break apart 56 in 3 different ways!

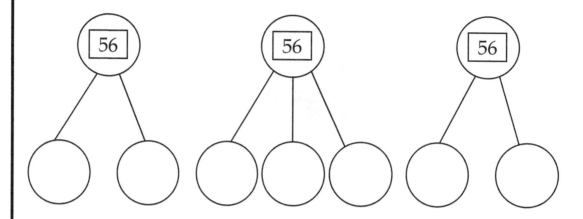

Thursday: Number Talk

Pick a number from each circle. Make a subtraction problem. Write the problem under the way you solved it. For example, 18 – 9. I can do that in my head because it is half fact.

Did I do it in my head?	Did I use a model?	Did I write down the numbers and solve it on paper?

A.

28   61
80   15   75
28   14   99
33   52
100   47   18

B.

18   19   8
17   25   63
9   10
12   36   44
57   7   11

Friday: Model That!

Jamal had 77 marbles. He had 2 more than Mike. How many did Mike have? How many did they have altogether?

Solve with a tape diagram.

Monday: Convince Me!

This routine is about getting students to defend and justify their thinking. Be sure to emphasize the language of reasoning. Students should focus on proving it with numbers, words, and pictures. They should say things like:

This is true! I can prove it with....
This is the same because....
I am going to use _____ to show my thinking.
I am going to defend my answer by _____.

Tuesday: Vocabulary Match

Say all the words together as a class and get students to think about if they know these words, if they are familiar, or if they are completely unfamiliar. Then, have students turn and work with their partners on the match. Come back together as a class and discuss the words.

* Note: It is important to call everyone back together at the end and talk about the vocabulary. Briefly go over the vocabulary, this is all second grade vocabulary.

Wednesday: Patterns/Skip Counting

These are open skip counting problems. Students should come up with their answers and share them with a partner, and then be ready to discuss them with the whole class.

Thursday: Number Strings

Students should discuss the string as a whole class. You want the emphasis to be on the relationships between the numbers. In this Number String students are thinking about what it means to subtract a 9. How do you adjust the number to make it an easier problem? So when we think about 42 – 29 we can add 1 to each number and make it an easier problem: 43 – 30. Practicing these strategies is important so that they become internalized in students' thinking.

Friday: Picture That!

Students use the picture as a springboard into an estimation story. This can be done as a whole class. The teacher is probably going to have to review what estimation means.

Week 9 Activities

Monday: Convince Me!

Convince me that
14 + 6 + 12 = 20 + 12

Tuesday: Vocabulary Match

Match the words with the definitions.

equal sign	+
less than	>
minus sign	<
greater than	–
plus sign	=

Wednesday: Patterns/Skip Counting

Name 2 numbers between 50 and 100 that you would say if you were skip counting by 2s.

Name 2 numbers greater than 150 that you would say if you were skip counting by 5s.

Name 2 numbers greater than 700 that you would say if you were skip counting by 10s.

Thursday: Number Strings

Discuss the number string. What do you notice?

$$12 - 9$$
$$22 - 9$$
$$42 - 29$$
$$62 - 39$$
$$73 - 49$$
$$84 - 59$$

Friday: Picture That!

Write an estimation story about a carton of oranges.

Week 10 Teacher Notes

Monday: Reasoning Matrices

Reasoning matrices are great. Students should read them and work on them with a partner and then share their thinking with the whole class.

Tuesday: Vocabulary Tic Tac Toe

These are quick partner energizers. Read all the words together. Then go! The students have 7 minutes to play the game. They play rock, paper, scissors to see who starts. They then take turns choosing words and explaining it to their partner. Then, they have to do a sketch or something to show they understand the word. Everybody should play the first game, if they have time, they can play the next one.

* Note: It is important to call everyone back together at the end and talk about the vocabulary. Briefly go over the vocabulary, this is all second grade vocabulary.

Wednesday: Number of the Day

Number of the Day is important and reviews place value skills. There are both closed and open items in the routine. Give the students about 5 minutes to work on this and discuss it with their math partner. Then, come back together as a class and talk about what the students did.

Thursday: Number Talk

This is a typical Number Talk where students are thinking about the ways in which they can solve this addition problem. You want students to think about partial sums, counting up, and compensation. Students should be focusing on different ways. They could make the 55 a 54 and the 49 a 50. They could also add the tens and then add the ones.

Friday: Write a Problem

In these problems students are given the equation and they have to write a story to match it. They should do this on their own and share it with their partner to see if their story makes sense. Then, they will discuss their thinking with the whole class.

Monday: Reasoning Matrices

	Lemon pie	Strawberry pie	Chocolate pie	Pumpkin pie	Cherry pie	Pecan pie
Jenny						
Jamal						
Miguel						
Kelly						
Maria						
Grace						

Use the clues to figure out who ate which pie. Jenny does not like fruit. Jamal loves nuts. Miguel loves fruit and hates chocolate. Kelly loves lemony tasting things. Maria loves fruit that grows on trees. Grace loves October and all the foods that we eat then.

Tuesday: Vocabulary Tic Tac Toe

Do rock, paper, scissors to decide who goes first. Pick a square. Write a description or draw a picture of the answer on the side. Then, put an x or o. If your partner disagrees, look it up. If the player is correct, they go again. If wrong, they lose the turn.

Use in an example. Write it down.

A.

<	+	greater than
>	–	less than
fewer	=	equal to

B.

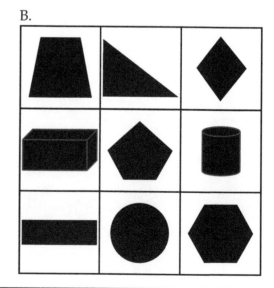

Wednesday: Number of the Day

Fill in the boxes.

247

Word form	10 more	10 less
Expanded form	_____ + _____ = 247	_____ − _____ = 247
Base ten sketch	How many more to 500?	Odd or even?
100 more	100 less	247 − _____ = _____

Thursday: Number Talk

What are some ways to solve 55 + 49?

Friday: Write a Problem

Tell a word problem about this equation:

$$25 + 35 = 60$$

Story:

Model:

Equation:

Week 11 Teacher Notes

Monday: Venn Diagram

Students read the labels for the two circles and the overlap and then fill them in accordingly.

Tuesday: Vocabulary Bingo

Students put each of the words in a box in a different order than they appear. When the teacher calls a word, the students should cover it. Whoever gets 4 in a row vertically, horizontally, or any of the 4 corners, wins. The teacher should call the word, give a definition or show an illustration.

Wednesday: Why Is It Not?

Students look at each problem and think about why the given answer is not correct. They have to discuss it and then explain their thinking to the class.

Thursday: Number Talk

Students pick a number from each circle and make an addition problem. They should write the problem under the way they solved it. For example, "I can do that in my head. I added 165 and 29. I made the problem 164 and 30 and I got 194."

Friday: What's the Question?

Students need to read the problem 3 times. First they should read the problem and think about the story. Then, they should read the problem and think about the numbers. Then, they should read the story and think about questions that they could ask.

Monday: Venn Diagram

Look at the circles. Fill in the Venn diagram.

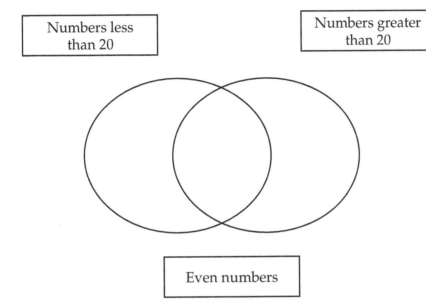

Tuesday: Vocabulary Bingo

Put each of the words in a box in a different order than they appear. Play bingo. When the teacher calls a word, cover it. Whoever gets 4 in a row vertically, horizontally, or diagonally between any 4 corners wins.

Words: array, multiplication, division, divisor, bar graph, centimeter, column, row, equal group, category, data, factor, product, sum, difference, addend.
Write a word in each space.

Wednesday: Why Is It Not?

Think about it. Talk about it with a partner. Share with the class.

14 = ____ + 6 Why is it not 20?	Why is this not a polygon? 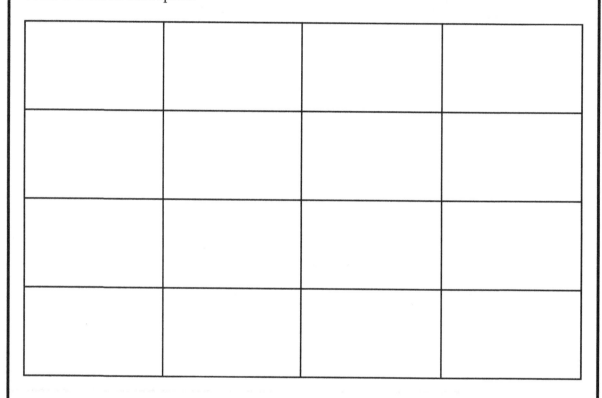

Thursday: Number Talk

Pick a number from each circle. Make an addition problem. Write the problem under the way you solved it. For example, "I can do that in my head. I added 165 and 29. I made the problem 164 and 30 and I got 194."

Did I do it in my head?	Did I use a model?	Did I write down the numbers and solve it on paper?

A.

138   142
165   378
284   199
523   457
350   77

B.

38   29   5
   26   14   17
11   2   0
   9   10   8   5

Friday: What's the Question?

Read the problem 3 times. First read the problem and think about the story. Then read the problem and think about the numbers. Finally, read the story and think about questions you could ask.

The bakery had 25 lemon cookies, 33 sugar cookies and 17 chocolate chip cookies.	What are some questions that you can ask?

Week 12 Teacher Notes

Monday: Legs and Feet

These are reasoning problems. Students look at the first picture and then reason through the next problems using the first picture as a launchpad.

Tuesday: Vocabulary Brainstorm

In each thought cloud students write or draw something that has to do with fractions.

Wednesday: 3 Truths and a Fib

Students have to read the statements and decide which 3 are true and which one is not. They then discuss with their neighbor which one is false. They must explain their thinking to their neighbor and then to the class.

Thursday: Number Talk

Students discuss the expression and talk about ways to solve the problem.

Friday: Word Problem Sort

Students have to figure out which one of the problems is a compare problem and what type of compare problem it is.

Week 12 Activities

Monday: Legs and Feet

There is a chicken and a cow.

A. How many legs? 	B. If there are 10 legs and there has to be a chicken and a cow, how many animals and what type could there be?
C. If there are 12 legs and there has to be a chicken and a cow, how many animals and what type could there be?	D. If there are 14 legs and there has to be a chicken and a cow, how many animals and what type could there be?

Tuesday: Vocabulary Brainstorm

Fractions – In each thought cloud write or draw something that has to do with fractions.

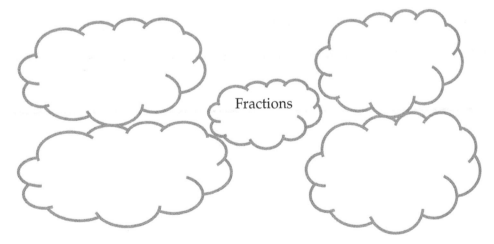

Fractions

Wednesday: 3 Truths and a Fib

Read the statements and decide which 3 are true and which one is not. Think about why it is not true. Explain your thinking to your neighbor and then the group.

90 can be 9 tens	90 can be 5 tens and 40 ones
90 can be 90 fives	90 can be 8 tens and 10 ones

Thursday: Number Talk

What are some ways to solve 100 – 28?

Friday: Word Problem Sort

Circle the compare problem. How do you know it is a compare problem? Are you looking for the bigger part, the smaller part, or the difference? Solve all 3 problems.

A. Luke has 25 red marbles and 17 green ones. How many does he have altogether?

B. Maria has 45 marbles. She has 22 more than her sister. How many does her sister have?

C. Jamal had 30 marbles. His sister gave him 3 more. How many does he have now?

Monday: What Doesn't Belong?

Students have to choose the item that doesn't belong in the set.

Tuesday: Frayer Model

Students have to fill in the different boxes about multiplication.

Wednesday: Round That!

Students have to choose numbers that match the criteria.

Thursday: Number Talk

Students discuss ways to solve the expression.

Friday: What's the Question?

Students have to read the problem 3 times. The first time they should think about the story. The second time, they should think about the numbers. The third time they should think about which questions they could ask. They have to think of at least 2 questions they could ask about this story. They then have to write them down, solve them, and discuss them with a classmate.

Monday: What Doesn't Belong?

Choose the item that doesn't belong in each set.

A.

add	difference
sum	altogether

B.

$100 - 75$	$75 - 50$
$5 + 5 + 5 + 5 + 5$	$90 - 50$

Tuesday: Frayer Model

Fill in the boxes.

Multiplication

Definition	Examples
Give a picture example	Non-examples

Wednesday: Round That!

Prove it with numbers, words, and/or pictures!

A. What are 3 numbers that round to 50?

B. What are 3 numbers that round to 700?

Thursday: Number Talk

What are some ways to think about and represent:

$$5 \times 7$$

Friday: What's the Question?

Read the problem 3 times. The first time think about the story. The second time, think about the numbers. The third time think about which questions you could ask.

Think of at least 2 questions you could ask about this story. Write them down. Solve them. Discuss with your classmates.

Mary has 2 boxes with 4 red marbles in each box and 2 boxes with 2 blue marbles in each box.

1)

2)

Week 14 Teacher Notes

Monday: Always, Sometimes, Never

Students should discuss the statement and decide if it is always, sometimes, or never true.

Tuesday: Frayer Model

Students have to fill in the different boxes about division.

Wednesday: Guess My Number

Students have to read the riddle. They should think about the clues and discuss what they think the answer is with a classmate.

Thursday: Number Talk

Students discuss ways to solve the expression.

Friday: Picture That!

Students have to write a multiplication problem about the picture.

Week 14 Activities

Monday: Always, Sometimes, Never

Read the statement and decide if it is always, sometimes, or never true. Justify your thinking with numbers, words, and/or pictures.

A.

When you subtract, the difference is less than the number you started with.

B.

If you halve a number, the number is always even.

Tuesday: Frayer Model

Fill in the boxes.

Division

Definition	Examples
Give a picture example	Non-examples

Wednesday: Guess My Number

Read the riddle. Think about the clues. Discuss what you think the answer is with a classmate.

A.

I am a 2-digit number.
I am greater than 47 and less than 89.
I am odd.
If you skip count by 5s you will say my number.
The sum of my digits is greater than 11 and less than 13.
What number am I?

B.

I am a 2-digit number.
I am less than 100.
I am greater than 8 x 10.
I am less than 9 x 10.
I am an even number.
The difference between my digits is 2.
What number am I?

Thursday: Number Talk

What are some ways to think about and show:

2 x 8
4 x 8
8 x 8

Friday: Picture That!

Write a multiplication problem about the picture.

Story:

Model:

Equation:

Week 15 Teacher Notes

Monday: It Is/It Isn't

In this routine you want students to be focusing on the vocabulary. Encourage students to use the word bank. This is a scaffold only though. This is to get them started. The conversation might sound something like this: "It is partitioning. It is not adding."

Tuesday: Vocabulary Fill-in

Students fill in the blanks with the words from the word bank.

Wednesday: Venn Diagram

Students read the labels for the two circles and the overlap and then fill them in accordingly.

Thursday: Number Talk

In this Number Talk you want the students to discuss their thinking with strategies and models. Ask students about the strategies that they might use.

Friday: What's the Question?

Students have to read the problem 3 times. The first time they should think about the story. The second time, they should think about the numbers. The third time they should think about which questions they could ask. They have to think of at least 2 questions they could ask about this story. They then have to write them down, solve them, and discuss them with a classmate.

Week 15 Activities

Monday: It Is/It Isn't

Describe what the word is and isn't.

Division

It Is	It Isn't

Tuesday: Vocabulary Fill-in

Fill in the blank spaces with the word bank vocabulary.

Word bank: multiplication, division, array, product, quotient

A. The answer to a multiplication problem is called the _____.

B. Repeated addition can show _____.

C. _____ can be breaking something apart equally and sharing it out.

D. Equal groups of rows and columns make an _____.

E. The answer to a division problem is called the _____.

Wednesday: Venn Diagram

Look at the circles. Fill in the Venn diagram.

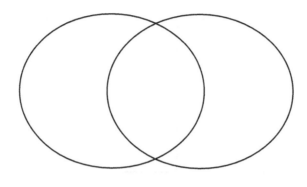

2-digit numbers

3-digit numbers

Even numbers

Thursday: Number Talk

What are some ways to think about and show:

$$4 \div 2$$
$$8 \div 2$$
$$6 \div 2$$
$$10 \div 2$$
$$12 \div 2$$

Friday: What's the Question?

Think of at least 2 questions you could ask about this story. Write them down. Discuss with your classmates.

The Parkers went on vacation. On Monday they drove 125 miles. On Tuesday they drove 300 miles. On Wednesday they drove 299 miles.

1)

2)

Monday: What Doesn't Belong?

When doing What Doesn't Belong?, have the students do the calculations (in their journals, on scratch paper, or on the activity page). Then, have them share their thinking with a friend. Finally, pull them back to the group.

Tuesday: 1-Minute Essay/Quick Write

Give students the designated part of the time to write everything they can about multiplication and then share and then write again and finally share out with the class.

Wednesday: Fraction of the Day

Students fill in the boxes to represent the fraction of the day.

Thursday: Number Talk

Students pick a number from each circle and multiply the numbers. They should decide how they will solve it and write that expression under the title.

Friday: Word Problem Sort

Students read and sort the problems. They have to underline the multiplication problem and circle the division problem. They should answer both of them and explain their thinking to their partner.

Week 16 Activities

Monday: What Doesn't Belong?

Choose the item that doesn't belong in each set.

A.

$10 \div 10$	$100 \div 10$
$50 \div 5$	$20 \div 2$

B.

5×7	$(2 \times 5) + (5 \times 5)$
$2 \times 2 \times 7$	7×5

Tuesday: 1-Minute Essay/Quick Write

(For 30 seconds) Write everything you can about multiplication. Use numbers, words, and pictures.

(15 seconds) Now switch with a neighbor and add 1 thing to their list.

(15 seconds) Now add 1 more thing to your list.

Wednesday: Fraction of the Day

Fill in the boxes to represent the fraction of the day.

$$\frac{1}{4}$$

Word form	Rectangle model
Circle model	Draw a line and cut it into 4 equal parts

Thursday: Number Talk

Pick a number from each circle. Multiply them. Decide how you will solve it and write that expression under the title.

Did I do it in my head?	Did I use a model?	Did I write down the numbers and solve it on paper?

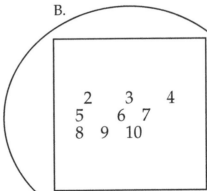

A.

2 3 4
5 6 7
8 9 10

B.

2 3 4
5 6 7
8 9 10

Friday: Word Problem Sort

Underline the problem that describes a multiplication situation. Circle the problem that describes a division situation. Answer both of them. Explain your thinking to your partner.

A. Dave had 12 marbles. He gave an equal amount to his 3 brothers. How many did each brother get?

B. Dave had 12 marbles. He got 2 more boxes with 5 marbles in each box. How many marbles does he have now?

Monday: Input/Output Table

Students must fill in the empty boxes according to the rule.

Tuesday: Vocabulary Tic Tac Toe

These are quick partner energizers. Read all the words together. Then go! The students have 7 minutes to play the game. They play rock, paper, scissors to see who starts. They then take turns choosing words and explaining it to their partner. Then, they have to do a sketch or something to show they understand the word. Everybody should play the first game, if they have time, they can play the next one.

*Note: It is important to call everyone back together at the end and talk about the vocabulary. Briefly go over the vocabulary.

Wednesday: What Doesn't Belong?

When doing What Doesn't Belong?, have the students do the calculations (in their journals, on scratch paper, or on the activity page). Then, have them share their thinking with a friend. Finally, pull them back to the group.

Thursday: Number Strings

Students have to think about the expression and discuss which strategies they would use to solve it.

Friday: Word Problem Fill-in

Students choose their own problem. They fill in the blanks to make their own problem and then solve it.

Monday: Input/Output Table

Fill in the empty boxes according to the rule.

What's the rule?		What's the rule?		Make your own....	
In	**Out**	**In**	**Out**	**In**	**Out**
2	10	14	7		
3	15	10	5		
4	20	16	8		
5		8			
6			3		
	35		2		

Tuesday: Vocabulary Tic Tac Toe

Do rock, paper, scissors to decide who goes first. Pick a square. Write a description or draw a picture of the answer on the side. Then, put an x or o. If your partner disagrees, look it up. If the player is correct, they go again. If wrong, they lose the turn.

quotient	dividend	product		rounding	division	multiplication
difference	factor	sum		yards	centimeters	thousands
multiplication	divisor	addend		inches	divisor	tape diagram

Wednesday: What Doesn't Belong?

Choose the item that doesn't belong in each set.

A.

49	51
54	42

B.

99	102
94	96

Thursday: Number Strings

Discuss the number string. What do you notice?

2 x 2	2 x 5	2 x 7
4 x 2	4 x 5	4 x 7
8 x 2	8 x 5	8 x 7

Friday: Word Problem Fill-in

Fill in the blanks to make your own problem. Solve it.

Mike had _____ marbles. He gave _____ friends an equal amount. How many marbles did each friend get?

    (6 or 12)   (2 or 3)

Week 18 Teacher Notes

Monday: True or False?

Students read the statements and decide if they are true or false. They then write that in the box. In the third column, they should make their own statement.

Tuesday: What Doesn't Belong?

When doing What Doesn't Belong?, have the students do the calculations (in their journals, on scratch paper, or on the activity page). Then, have them share their thinking with a friend. Finally, pull them back to the group.

Wednesday: Guess My Number

Students have to read the riddle. They should think about the clues and discuss what they think the answer is with a classmate.

Thursday: Number Talk

Students have to think about the expression and discuss which strategies they would use to solve it.

Friday: Picture That!

Students look at the picture and write an estimation story about it.

Monday: True or False?

Read the expressions and decide if they are true or false. Write that in the box. In the third column, make up your own.

1. True or False?	2. True or False?	3. Make your own and share it out
4 x 7 = 20 + 2 + 6	63 ÷ 9 = (3 x 2) + 2	

Tuesday: What Doesn't Belong?

Choose the item that doesn't belong in each set.

A.

quotient	dividend
product	divisor

B.

inches	milliliters
yards	centimeters

Wednesday: Guess My Number

Read the riddle. Think about the clues. Discuss what you think the answer is with a classmate.

A.	B.
I am a 2-digit number.	I am a 2-digit number.
I am greater than 5 x 8 and less than 6 x 10.	I am less than 20.
If you skip count by 4s you will say my number.	I am greater than 2 x 7.
	I am not odd.
The sum of my digits is greater than 10 and less than 12.	The sum of my digits is 9.
What number am I?	What number am I?

Thursday: Number Talk

What are some ways to think about:

$$7 \times 8$$

Friday: Picture That!

Write an estimation story about strawberries in boxes. Draw a model and write an equation that you could use to solve your story problem.

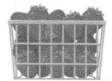    

Story:

Model:

Equation:

Monday: Break It up!

Students have to break up the problem and discuss how they did it with a partner.

Tuesday: 1-Minute Essay/Quick Write

Give students the designated part of the time to write everything they can about division and then share and then write again and finally share out with the class.

Wednesday: How Many More to

Students have to write how many more to each number from the start number.

Thursday: Number Talk

Students pick a number from each circle and make an addition problem. They should write the problem under the way they solved it. For example, "I can do that in my head. I added 350 and 50. I added 50 and 50 to make 100 and then 300 more which makes 400."

Friday: What's the Story?

Students have to write a story about the tape diagram.

Monday: Break It up!

Sketch the expression. Next, break it apart and then discuss what you did with your math partner.

3 x 7

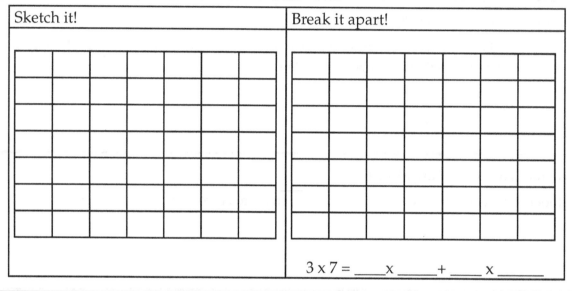

Sketch it!	Break it apart!

3 x 7 = _____ x _____ + _____ x _____

Tuesday: 1-Minute Essay/Quick Write

(For 30 seconds) Write everything you can about division. Use numbers, words, and pictures.

(15 seconds) Now switch with a neighbor and add 1 thing to their list.

(15 seconds) Now add 1 more thing to your list.

Wednesday: How Many More to

Write how many more to each number from the start number.

Start at 50 ... How many more to 100?
Start at 78 ... How many more to 100?
Start at 150 ... How many more to 200?
Start at 275 ... How many more to 500?
Start at 300 ... How many more to 1,000?

Thursday: Number Talk

Pick a number from each circle. Make an addition equation. Write the problem under the way you solved it. For example, 312 + 50. I can do that in my head.

Did I do it in my head?	Did I use a model?	Did I write down the numbers and solve it on paper?

A.

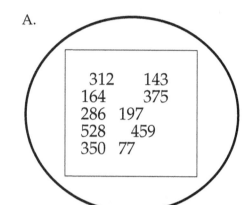

B.

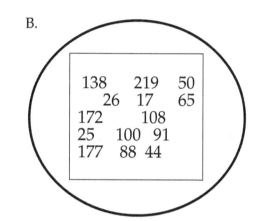

Friday: What's the Story?

Tell a story to match this tape diagram. Write an equation. Solve it.

3	3	3	3	3	3

Monday: True or False?

Students read the expressions and decide if they are true or false. They then write that in the space. In the final row they should make their own expression.

Tuesday: Vocabulary Brainstorm

Students have to fill in each thought cloud with information about area.

Wednesday: Find and Fix the Error

Students have to look at and think about the problem. They should decide what is wrong and fix it. Then discuss the work with a math partner.

Thursday: Number Talk

This is a typical Number Talk where students are thinking about the ways in which they can solve this subtraction problem. You want students to think about partial sums, counting up, and compensation. Students should be focusing on different ways.

Friday: What's the Story?

Students tell a division story to match this tape diagram. They should write an equation that represents the model.

Monday: True or False?

Read the expressions. Decide if they are true or false. Write it in the space.

	True or False?
5 + 10 = 3 x 5	
16/8 = 2 x 8	
34 + 16 = 100 – 50	
2 x 7 = 70 – 56	
Make your own!	

Tuesday: Vocabulary Brainstorm

In each thought cloud write or draw something that has to do with area.

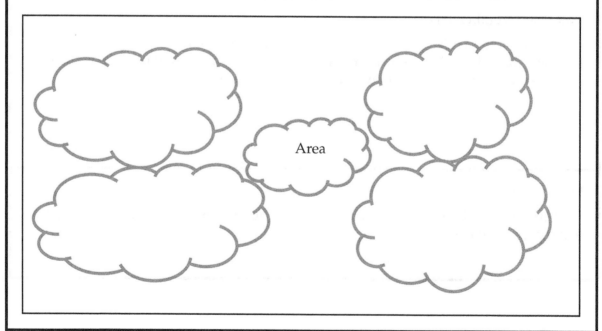

Area

Wednesday: Find and Fix the Error

Look at and think about the problem. Decide what is wrong and fix it. Then discuss the work with a math partner.

Luke did this...

```
  200
-  99
  299
```

What did he get wrong? How can he fix it?

Thursday: Number Talk

What are some ways to think about this problem:

$$500 - 298?$$

Friday: What's the Story?

Tell a story to match this tape diagram. Write an equation that represents the model.

5	5	5	5

Story:

Equation:

Week 21 Teacher Notes

Monday: Alike and Different

Students have to discuss how these shapes are alike and different.

Tuesday: Vocabulary Bingo

Students put each of the words in a box in a different order than they appear. When the teacher calls a word, the students should cover it. Whoever gets 4 in a row vertically, horizontally, or any of the 4 corners, wins. The teacher should call the word, give a definition or show an illustration.

Wednesday: Number Bond It!

Students have to show how to break apart a liter in 3 different ways. The note that 1,000 ml makes a liter is there so that students can think about different ways to break that apart.

Thursday: Number Talk

Students pick a number from each circle and multiply the numbers. They should decide how they will solve it and write that expression under the title.

Friday: What's the Story?

Students are given the answer. They have to write a story.

Week 21 Activities

Monday: Alike and Different

Discuss how these shapes are alike and different.

Tuesday: Vocabulary Bingo

Put each of the words in a box in a different order than they appear. Play bingo. When the teacher calls a word, cover it. Whoever gets 4 in a row vertically, horizontally, or any 4 corners, wins.

Place the words in different parts of the board.

Write a word in each space. Area, tape diagram, partial product, horizontal, centimeter, vertical, kilogram, gram, classify, parallelogram, quadrilateral, partial quotient, partial sums, partial differences, liter, milliliter.

Wednesday: Number Bond It!

1 liter = 1,000 ml
Show how to break apart a liter in 3 different ways.

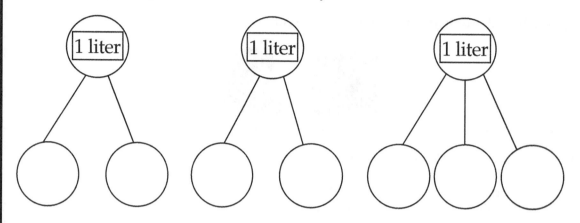

Thursday: Number Talk

Pick a number from each circle. Make a multiplication problem. Write the problem under the way you solved it.

Did I do it in my head?	Did I use a model?	Did I write down the numbers and solve it on paper?

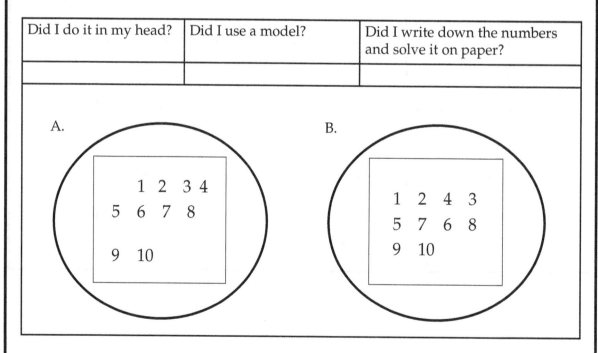

A.

1 2 3 4
5 6 7 8

9 10

B.

1 2 4 3
5 7 6 8
9 10

Friday: What's the Story?

Write a story where the quotient is 3 cookies.

Monday: Elapsed Time

Students have to tell the times that could be in the story given the criteria.

Tuesday: Frayer Model

Students have to fill in the boxes.

Wednesday: Fraction of the Day

Students have to fill in the boxes to represent the fraction.

Thursday: Number Talk

In this Number Talk you want the students to discuss their thinking with strategies and models. Ask students about the strategies that they might use.

Friday: What's the Story?

Students have to read the graph and then make up a story about what the data represents and tell it to their partner. They have to explain their thinking and be ready to share their thinking with the whole group.

Week 22 Activities

Monday: Elapsed Time

Read the story and tell what time Harry could have left and come back to his house.

Harry left his house to play basketball. He was gone for 45 minutes. What time could he have left? What time could he have come back?

Tuesday: Frayer Model

Fill in the boxes.

Rounding

Definition	Examples
Real life situation	Non-examples

Wednesday: Fraction of the Day

Fill in the boxes to represent the fraction.

$$\frac{1}{2}$$

Word form	Picture form
Plot it on the number line	Is it greater or less than $\frac{1}{4}$ How do you know?
$\longleftrightarrow$	

Thursday: Number Talk

What are some ways to think about and show:

$$10 \times 1$$
$$5 \times 1$$
$$10 \times 2$$
$$5 \times 2$$
$$10 \times 5$$
$$5 \times 5$$
$$10 \times 7$$
$$5 \times 7$$

Friday: What's the Story?

| Here's the graph. | What's the story? Make up a story about what the data represents and tell it to your partner. Ask some questions about the graph. Answer them. Explain your thinking. Be ready to share your thinking with the whole group. |

Here's the graph.

```
                        x
            x           x
      x     x           x
      x     x     x     x
x     x     x     x     x
x     x     x     x     x
½     1     1½    2     2½
```

Monday: Missing Number

Students must look at the missing numbers. They need to fill in what is missing and explain their thinking with a math partner.

Tuesday: Frayer Model

Students have to fill in the different boxes to represent the word.

Wednesday: What's Missing?

Students have to fill in the missing numbers.

Thursday: Number Talk

Students discuss ways to solve the expression.

Friday: Model That!

Students have to model the problem with a tape diagram.

Week 23 Activities

Monday: Missing Number

Look at the missing numbers. Fill in what is missing and explain your thinking to your math partner.

A. $3 \times \underline{} = 9$.

Lucy said the answer was 3. Michael said the answer was 27. Who is correct? Why?

Solve these:

B. $20 = 5 \times \underline{}$

C. $100 \div 10 = ?$

D. $6 \times \underline{} = 42$

Tuesday: Frayer Model

Fill in the boxes.

Area

Definition	Examples
Give a picture example	Non-examples

Wednesday: What's Missing?

Fill in the missing numbers.

A. 7____, _____, 28, 35, 42, _____, _____ , _____

B. 8000, 4000, _____, 1000 _____, 250, _____

C. Make your own pattern:

_____, _____, _____, _____, _____, _____, _____

Thursday: Number Talk

What could you do if you don't know the answer to 5 x 7?

Friday: Model That!

In the aquarium there were 10 animals. Five were turtles and the rest were fish. Then, 7 more fish swam up. How many fish are there now? How many animals are there altogether?

Model it with a tape diagram.

Week 24 Teacher Notes

Monday: Input/Output Table

Students have to create an input/output table where the rule is to multiply by 7.

Tuesday: 1-Minute Essay/Quick Write

Students have 1 minute to write everything they can about fractions using numbers, words, and pictures.

Wednesday: Round That!

Students have to name 3 numbers that round to the designated number.

Thursday: Number Talk

Students pick a number from each circle and divide the numbers. They should decide how they will solve it and write that expression under the title.

Friday: Model That!

Students have to read, model, and solve the word problem.

Monday: Input/Output Table

Create an input/output table where the rule is to multiply by 7.

In	Out

Tuesday: 1-Minute Essay/Quick Write

You have 1 minute to write everything you know about fractions. Use numbers, words, and pictures.

Go!

Wednesday: Round That!

Name 3 numbers that round to 800.

Thursday: Number Talk

Pick a number from each circle. Divide them. Decide how you will solve it and write that expression under the title.

Did I do it in my head?	Did I use a model?	Did I write down the numbers and solve it on paper?

A.

28 10   18

24   12 27

40 36 48

14   21   45

B.

1 2 3

4 5 6

7 8 9

Friday: Model That!

At the butterfly museum there were 40 insects in the garden. Half of the insects were butterflies and the other half were ladybugs. Then, some more butterflies came, and now there are 80 butterflies. How many butterflies came? How many insects are there altogether now?

Model:

Equation:

Answer:

Week 25 Teacher Notes

Monday: What Doesn't Belong?

When doing What Doesn't Belong?, have the students do the calculations (in their journals, on scratch paper, or on the activity page). Then, have them share their thinking with a friend. Finally, pull them back to the group.

Tuesday: Vocabulary Tic Tac Toe

These are quick partner energizers. Read all the words together. Then go! The students have 7 minutes to play the game. They play rock, paper, scissors to see who starts. They then take turns choosing words and explaining it to their partner. Then, they have to do a sketch or something to show they understand the word. Everybody should play the first game, if they have time, they can play the next one.

*Note: It is important to call everyone back together at the end and talk about the vocabulary. Briefly go over the vocabulary.

Wednesday: Fraction of the Day

Students have to fill in the boxes to represent the fraction.

Thursday: Number Talk

In this Number Talk you want the students to discuss their thinking with strategies and models. Ask students about the strategies that they might use.

Friday: Model That!

Students have to read, model, and solve the word problem.

Week 25 Activities

Monday: What Doesn't Belong?

Choose the item that doesn't belong in each set.

A.

$25 \div 5$	$20 \div 4$
$16 - 9$	$30 - 25$

B.

$(3 \times 6) + (3 \times 3)$	$(3 \times 3) + (3 \times 3)$
$(3 \times 5) + (3 \times 4)$	3×9

Tuesday: Vocabulary Tic Tac Toe

Do rock, paper, scissors to decide who goes first. Pick a square. Write a description or draw a picture of the answer on the side. Then, put an x or o. If your partner disagrees, look it up. If the player is correct, they go again. If wrong, they lose the turn.

A.

fraction	mixed number	factor
divisor	quotient	product
equation	equivalent	dividend

B.

mass	parallel	intersecting
pounds	ounces	length
quart	pint	cup

Wednesday: Fraction of the Day

Fill in the boxes to represent the fraction.

$$\frac{3}{3}$$

Word form	Picture form
Plot it on the number line $\longleftrightarrow$	Is it greater or less than $\frac{6}{6}$? How do you know?

Thursday: Number Talk

What are the missing numbers?

```
   7 _ 8
-  _ 5 _
 ---------
   2 0 6
```

Friday: Model That!

Mr. Lucas had 1 piece of wood that was 25 ft. long. He cut bookshelves that were 5ft. long. How many did he cut?

Model with a tape diagram:

Week 26 Teacher Notes

Monday: Number Line It!

Students have to plot the fractions on the number line from least to greatest.

Tuesday: Vocabulary Match

Often when reviewing vocabulary it is good to review the grade level words mixed, meaning not by a specific category. Students should say the word and then find the matching definition. They should have some minutes to do this on their own and then an opportunity to go over their thinking with their math partner. Then, after about 5 minutes, bring them back together as a group and discuss the thinking. Ask students which words were tricky and which ones were easy. Also ask them if there were any that they didn't recognize, that they have never seen before. Have them draw a little sketch by each word so as to help them remember the word.

Wednesday: Fraction of the Day

Students have to fill in the boxes to represent the fraction.

Thursday: Find and Fix the Error

Students have to look at and think about the problem. They should decide what is wrong and fix it. Then discuss the work with a math partner.

Friday: What's the Story?

Students have to write a story to match the model.

Week 26 Activities

Monday: Number Line It!

Plot these on the number line in order as accurately as possible.

$$\frac{1}{8}, \quad \frac{1}{2}, \quad \frac{3}{4}, \quad \frac{4}{4}, \quad \frac{3}{8}$$

Tuesday: Vocabulary Match

Match the words with the definitions.

equivalent	the part that names the pieces of the whole that we are considering
quotient	to break apart
denominator	the same as the answer to a division problem
numerator	names the
decompose	number of parts in the whole

Wednesday: Fraction of the Day

Fill in the boxes.

$$\frac{5}{4}$$

Word form	Draw a model

Plot it on the number line

Thursday: Find and Fix the Error

What are the missing numbers?

$$
\begin{array}{r}
\_\ 7\ 5 \\
-\ 2\ 3\ \_ \\
\hline
4\ \_\ 2 \\
\end{array}
$$

Why is it wrong?

What did he do wrong?

How can we fix it?

Friday: What's the Story?

Write a story to match the model.

2	2	2	2	2

Week 27 Teacher Notes

Monday: Always, Sometimes, Never

Students should discuss the statement and decide if it is always, sometimes, or never true.

Tuesday: Frayer Model

Students have to fill in the different boxes to represent the word.

Wednesday: Patterns/Skip Counting

Students have to look at the pattern and figure out what comes next. They should be ready to discuss their thinking with a math partner.

Thursday: Number Talk

This is an open number talk. Students have to come up with ways to make a sum. You want students to think about partial sums, counting up and compensation. Students should be focusing on different ways. For example: $350 + 250 + 80$.

Friday: Equation Match

Students have to match the problem with the equation.

Monday: Always, Sometimes, Never

Discuss the statement and decide if it is always, sometimes, or never true.

If you multiply a number by 1 you always get that number.

Prove it with numbers, words, and pictures.

Tuesday: Frayer Model

Fill in the boxes.

Fourths

Definition	Examples
Give a picture example	**Non-examples**

Wednesday: Patterns/Skip Counting

Complete and describe the following patterns:

1. 1,600, ___, ___, 200, 100, 50, _____

2. 2, 4, _____, 16, 32, _____, _____, _____

3. Make your own:

   ____, _____, _____, _____, _____, _____, _____, ____

Thursday: Number Talk

Name 3 different problems that have 3 addends that **almost** add to 700.

Friday: Equation Match

You have to match the problem with the equation.

$$350 - m = 12$$

Problem A	Problem B
The bakery had 350 cupcakes. They sold 12. How many do they have left?	The bakery had 350 cupcakes. They sold some. They have 12 left. How many did they sell?

Week 28 Teacher Notes

Monday: Why Is It Not?

Students look at each problem and think about why the given answer is not correct. They have to discuss it and then explain their thinking to the class.

Tuesday: It Is/It Isn't

In this routine you want students to be focusing on the vocabulary. Encourage students to use the word bank. This is a scaffold only though.

Wednesday: Number of the Day

Students fill in the boxes to represent the number of the day.

Thursday: Number Talk

Students pick a number from each circle and multiply the numbers. They should decide how they will solve it and write that expression under the title.

Friday: What's the Story?

Students have to write a story that matches the model.

Monday: Why Is It Not?

Think about it and share it with a partner. Share with the class.

A. 250 + ____ = 300

Why is it not 550?

B. 3 x ___ = 10

Why is it not 30?

Tuesday: It Is/It Isn't

Describe what the word is and isn't.

789

It Is	It Isn't

Vocabulary bank: more than, less than, greater than, digits, odd, even.

Wednesday: Number of the Day

Fill in the boxes.

5,109

Word form	10 more	10 less
Expanded form	_____ + _____ = 5,109	_____ – _____ = 5,109
100 more	How many more to 10,000?	Odd or even
1,000 more	100 less	5,109 – _____ = _____

Thursday: Number Talk

Pick a number from each circle. Make a multiplication problem. Write the problem under the way you solved it.

Did I do it in my head?	Did I use a model?	Did I write down the numbers and solve it on paper?

A.

```
1  2  3
4  5  6

7  8  9
10   0
```

B.

```
1  2  3
4  5  6

7  8  9
10   0
```

Friday: What's the Story?

Write a story that matches the model.

210

210	10

Week 29 Teacher Notes

Monday: Reasoning about Numbers

Students have to reason about the numbers in the problem.

Tuesday: Vocabulary Fill-in

Students fill in the blank spaces with the word bank vocabulary.

Wednesday: Guess My Number

Students have to read the riddle. They should think about the clues and discuss what they think the answer is with a classmate.

Thursday: Number Talk

This is a typical Number Talk where students are thinking about the ways in which they can solve this subtraction problem. You want students to think about partial sums, counting up, and compensation. Students should be focusing on different ways.

Friday: Word Problem Sort

Students have to sort the word problems and find the compare problem and defend their thinking.

Week 29 Activities

Monday: Reasoning about Numbers

A. Name 2 numbers that almost make 1,000 when you add them.

B. Name 2 numbers that almost make 1,000 when you subtract them.

Tuesday: Vocabulary Fill-in

Fill in the blank spaces with the word bank vocabulary.

Word bank: addition, sum, difference, fraction

The answer to an _____ problem is called the _____.

The answer to a subtraction problem is called the_____.

A _____ is a part of a number.

Wednesday: Guess My Number

Read the riddle. Think about the clues. Discuss what you think the answer is with a classmate.

I am greater than 10 x 10.

I am less than 150 – 42.

I am not an odd number.

If you skip count by 3s you will say my number.

What number am I?

Thursday: Number Talk

What are some ways to solve 201 − 199?

Friday: Word Problem Sort

Circle the compare problem. How do you know it is a compare problem? Are you looking for the bigger part, the smaller part, or the difference? Answer all the problems.

A. Luke has 10 red marbles and 17 green ones. How many does he have altogether?

B. Maria has 24 marbles. She has 12 more than her sister. How many does her sister have?

C. Jamal had 30 marbles. His sister gave him 10 more. How many does he have now?

Monday: 2 Arguments

Students have to read both arguments and decide which one they agree with. They need to justify their thinking with numbers, words, and/or pictures.

Tuesday: Vocabulary Bingo

Students put each of the words in a box in a different order than they appear. When the teacher calls a word, the students should cover it. Whoever gets 4 in a row vertically, horizontally, or any of the 4 corners, wins. The teacher should call the word, give a definition or show an illustration.

Wednesday: Number Line It!

Students have to plot the numbers from least to greatest.

Thursday: Number Talk

Students pick a number from each circle and make a division problem. They should write the problem under the way they solved it. For example, "I can do that in my head. 14 divided by 7 is 2. I know this because 2 x 7 is 14."

Friday: What's the Question?

Students have to read the problem 3 times. The first time they should think about the story. The second time, they should think about the numbers. The third time they should think about which questions they could ask. They have to think of at least 2 questions they could ask about this story. They then have to write them down, solve them, and discuss them with a classmate.

Monday: 2 Arguments

$$24 \div \underline{} = 6$$

John said the answer was 30.

Maria said the answer was 4.

Who do you agree with?

Why?

Tuesday: Vocabulary Bingo

Put each of the words in a box in a different order than they appear. Play bingo. When the teacher calls a word, cover it. Whoever gets 4 in a row vertically, horizontally, or any 4 corners wins.

Words: fourths, thirds, halves, denominator, numerator, whole, sum, difference, quotient, product, divisor, dividend, factor, fifths, sixths, equivalent.

Write a word in each space.

Wednesday: Number Line It!

Plot these numbers on the number line as accurately as possible.

$$499 \quad 900 \quad 250 \quad 5 \quad 750$$

0 ←――――――――――――――――――――――→ 1,000

Thursday: Number Talk

Pick a number from each circle. Make a division problem. Then, decide how you are going to solve it. Write the problem under the way you solved it.

Did I do it in my head?	Did I use a model?	Did I write down the numbers and solve it on paper?

12 14 16
18 21 15
24 40 30
27

1 3 5
2 4 6
8 10
9 7

Friday: What's the Question?

Read the problem 3 times. The first time think about the story. The second time, think about the numbers. The third time think about which questions you could ask. Ask at least 2 questions you could ask about this story. Write them down, solve them, and discuss them with a classmate.

The Smiths went on vacation. On Monday, they drove 109 miles. On Tuesday, they drove 78 miles. On Wednesday, they drove 59 miles.

Week 31 Teacher Notes

Monday: True or False?

Students read the statements and decide if they are true or false. They then explain their thinking.

Tuesday: Vocabulary Brainstorm

Students fill in the clouds with numbers, words, and pictures to discuss the target word.

Wednesday: 3 Truths and a Fib

Students have to read the statements and decide which 3 are true and which one is not. They then discuss with their neighbor which one is false. They must explain their thinking to their neighbor and then to the class.

Thursday: Number Talk

Students reason about numbers. They think about and explain patterns.

Friday: Model That!

Students have to read and model the problem.

Monday: True or False?

Decide if the statements are true or false. Explain your thinking.

1. All quadrilaterals are parallelograms.
2. All squares are rectangles.
3. All rectangles are squares.
4. Some quadrilaterals are not parallelograms.

Tuesday: Vocabulary Brainstorm

Measurement – In each thought cloud write or draw something that has to do with measurement.

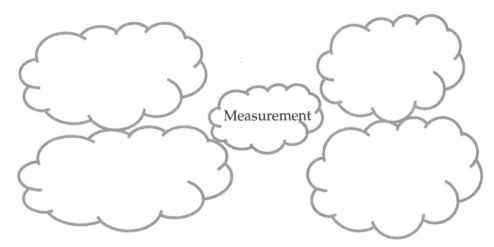

Wednesday: 3 Truths and a Fib

Which one is false? Why? Explain to your neighbor and then the group.

110 = 11 tens	110 = 110 tens
110 = 5 tens and 60 ones	110 = 10 tens and 10 ones

Thursday: Number Talk

Name some expressions that have a quotient of 10. Talk about any patterns that you notice.

Friday: Model That!

Model the problem.

Mary and Sue have candy bars that are the same size. If Mary ate $\frac{1}{2}$ of her candy bar and Sue at $\frac{2}{4}$ of her candy bar. Who ate more?	Draw it. Justify your thinking. Share with your neighbor and then the class.

Week 32 Teacher Notes

Monday: Reasoning about Numbers

Students have to reason about the problem and be ready to discuss it.

Tuesday: Vocabulary Bingo

Students put each of the words in a box in a different order than they appear. When the teacher calls a word, the students should cover it. Whoever gets 4 in a row vertically, horizontally, or any of the 4 corners, wins. The teacher should call the word, give a definition or show an illustration.

Wednesday: Greater Than, Less Than, in Between

Students have to look at the numbers and be ready to fill in the boxes using them.

Thursday: Number Talk

Students pick a number from each circle and multiply the numbers. They should decide how they will solve it and write that expression under the title.

Friday: What's the Question?

Students have to read the problem and then model it in 3 ways.

Week 32 Activities

Monday: Reasoning about Numbers

Draw 3 rectangles that could have an area of 24.

Explain your thinking to a neighbor. Be ready to discuss it with the whole class.

Tuesday: Vocabulary Bingo

Put each of the words in a box in a different order than they appear. Play bingo. When the teacher calls a word, cover it. Whoever gets 4 in a row vertically, horizontally, or any 4 corners wins.

Words: sphere, cone, hexagon, octagon, metric, mass, liter, ml, inch, cm, quotient, divisor, division, dividend, rectangular prism, quadrilateral.

Write a word in each space.

Wednesday: Greater Than, Less Than, in Between

Fill in the boxes based on the relationship about numbers.

777   5,891   1,000

Name a number that is greater than 777	Name a number that is greater than 5,891	Name a number that is greater than the sum of 5,891 and 777
Name a number that is less than 1,000	Name a number that is less than the difference between 1,000 and 777	Name a number in between 777 and 1,000

Thursday: Number Talk

Pick a number from each circle. Make a multiplication problem. Then, decide how you are going to solve it. Write the problem under the way you solved it.

Did I do it in my head?	Did I use a model?	Did I write down the numbers and solve it on paper?

1 2 4
3 5 6
7 8 9

10 20 30
40 50 60
70 80 90

Friday: What's the Question?

Read the problem and solve it in 3 ways.

Mica had 99 cents. She spent 20 cents. Show her change in 3 ways.

Way 1	Way 2	Way 3

Week 33 Teacher Notes

Monday: Reasoning about Numbers

Students have to reason about the problem and be ready to discuss it.

Tuesday: What Doesn't Belong?

When doing What Doesn't Belong?, have the students do the calculations (in their journals, on scratch paper or on the activity page). Then, have them share their thinking with a friend. Finally, pull them back to the group.

Wednesday: What Doesn't Belong?

When doing What Doesn't Belong?, have the students do the calculations (in their journals, on scratch paper or on the activity page). Then, have them share their thinking with a friend. Finally, pull them back to the group.

Thursday: Number Talk

Students should reason about different ways to solve this problem. There are various answers.

Friday: What's the Story?

Students look at the graph and make up a story and tell it to their partner. They must explain their thinking and be ready to share it with the whole group.

Week 33 Activities

Monday: Reasoning about Numbers

Explain your thinking to a neighbor. Be ready to discuss it with the whole class.

Ted and Joe both ate a candy bar. Ted said he ate $\frac{1}{2}$ of his. Joe said that he ate $\frac{1}{4}$ of his. Ted said that he ate more than Joe. Joe said he ate more than Ted. Who is correct and why?

Tuesday: What Doesn't Belong?

Choose the item that doesn't belong in each set.

A.

quadrilateral	trapezoid
rhombus	hexagon

B.

polygon	oval
parallelogram	pentagon

Wednesday: What Doesn't Belong?

Choose the item that doesn't belong in each set.

A.

1 hundred 5 tens 5 ones	15 tens 5 ones
1 hundred tens and 5 ones	155 ones

B.

20 x 9	60 + 60 + 60
200 – 20	150 + 20

Thursday: Number Talk

Name some different number pairs that have a difference of almost 75.

Explain your thinking to a partner.

Be able to defend your thinking in the whole group discussion.

Friday: What's the Story?

Here's the graph.	What's the story? Make up a story and tell it to your partner. Explain your thinking. Be ready to share your thinking to the whole group. Make up 3 questions and answer them.
  x x x x x x x x x _____ $\frac{1}{2}$ 1 $1\frac{1}{2}$ 2	

Monday: Convince Me!

This routine is about getting students to defend and justify their thinking. Be sure to emphasize the language of reasoning. Students should focus on proving it with numbers, words, and pictures. They should say things like:

This is true! I can prove it with….

This is the difference because….

I am going to use _____ to show my thinking.

I am going to defend my answer by _____.

Tuesday: Vocabulary Brainstorm

Students write about the word in the clouds using numbers, words, and pictures.

Wednesday: Find and Fix the Error

Students have to look at and think about the problem. They should decide what is wrong and fix it. Then discuss the work with a math partner.

Thursday: Number Talk

In this Number Talk you want the students to discuss their thinking with strategies and models. Ask students about the strategies that they might use. For example, students might make an easier problem by making 1299 and 5576 into 1300 and 5575.

Friday: What's the Question?

Students have to read the problem 3 times. The first time they should think about the story. The second time, they should think about the numbers. The third time they should think about which questions they could ask. They have to think of at least 2 questions they could ask about this story. They then have to write them down, solve them, and discuss them with a classmate.

Week 34 Activities

Monday: Convince Me!

Use numbers, words, and/or pictures.

Convince me that

$\frac{2}{2}$ = 1 whole

Tuesday: Vocabulary Brainstorm

Equivalent fractions – In each thought cloud write or draw something that has to do with equivalent fractions.

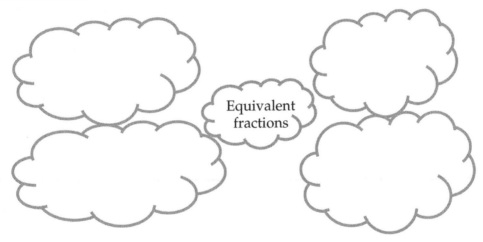

Equivalent fractions

Wednesday: Find and Fix the Error

Kevin solved the problem this way:

$$\begin{array}{r} 108 \\ + 79 \\ \hline 898 \end{array}$$

Why is it wrong?

What did he do wrong?

How can we fix it?

Thursday: Number Talk

What are some ways to solve 1299 + 5570?

Friday: What's the Question?

Think of at least 2 questions you could ask about this story. Write them down. Discuss with your classmates.

The jewelry store had 10 boxes with 2 gold rings in each box and 3 boxes with 4 silver rings in each box.

1)

2)

Week 35 Teacher Notes

Monday: 3 Truths and a Fib

Students have to read the statements and decide which 3 are true and which one is not. They then discuss with their neighbor which one is false. They must explain their thinking to their neighbor and then to the class.

Tuesday: Vocabulary Tic Tac Toe

These are quick partner energizers. Read all the words together. Then go! The students have 7 minutes to play the game. They play rock, paper, scissors to see who starts. They then take turns choosing words and explaining it to their partner. Then, they have to do a sketch or something to show they understand the word. Everybody should play the first game, if they have time, they can play the next one.

*Note: It is important to call everyone back together at the end and talk about the vocabulary. Briefly go over the vocabulary.

Wednesday: Number Bond It!

Students are working on decomposing numbers in different ways

Thursday: Number Talk

Students are choosing numbers and then discussing their different strategies.

Friday: Pattern That!

Students have to figure out what the pattern is. Then they have to make their own.

Monday: 3 Truths and a Fib

Which one is false? Why? Explain to your neighbor and then the group. Number the choices.

1. Centimeters measure length.
2. Liters measure liquid.
3. Kilometers measure mass.
4. Grams measure mass.

Tuesday: Vocabulary Tic Tac Toe

Do rock, paper, scissors to decide who goes first. Pick a square. Write a description or draw a picture of the answer on the side. Then, put an x or o. If your partner disagrees, look it up. If the player is correct, they go again. If wrong, they lose the turn.

line plot	picture graph	bar graph	area	perimeter	yard
fourths	halves	title	square	trapezoid	rectangle
categories	data	scale	polygon	quadrilateral	rhombus

Wednesday: Number Bond It!

Show how to break apart 74 in 3 different ways!

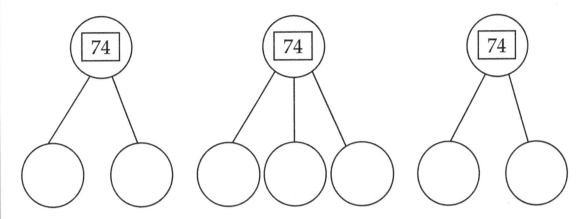

Thursday: Number Talk

Pick a number from each circle. Make an addition problem. Write the problem under the way you solved it.

Did I do it in my head?	Did I use a model?	Did I write down the numbers and solve it on paper?

A. Write five 2 or 3 digit numbers in this circle.   B.

10	100	58
22	35	41
67	79	88
99		

Friday: Pattern That!

Jamal wrote a pattern. His rule was to add 2, then multiply by 3. Which pattern below follows his rule?

Part A.

A. 0, 2, 4, 6, 8, 10.
B. 0, 2, 6, 8, 16, 20.
C. 0, 2, 6, 8, 24, 27.
D. None of the above.

Part B.

Make your own pattern that follows Jamal's rule.

Monday: True or False?

Students read the statement and think about if it is true or false. They then share their thinking with a friend and defend their answer. Finally, they should share their thinking with the whole group.

Tuesday: Vocabulary Bingo

Students put each of the words in a box in a different order than they appear. When the teacher calls a word, the students should cover it. Whoever gets 4 in a row vertically, horizontally, or any of the 4 corners, wins. The teacher should call the word, give a definition or show an illustration.

Wednesday: Guess My Number

Students have to read the riddle. They should think about the clues and discuss what they think the answer is with a classmate.

Thursday: Number Talk

Students pick a number from each circle and make an addition problem. They should write the problem under the way they solved it. For example, ". I can do that in my head. I added 165 and 29. I made the problem 164 and 30 and I got 194."

Friday: Make Your Own Problem

Students have to write their own problem.

Week 36 Activities

Monday: True or False?

A trapezoid is a parallelogram.

1. Think about it.
2. Share your thinking with a friend. Defend your answer.
3. Share your thinking with the group.

Tuesday: Vocabulary Bingo

Put each of the words in a box in a different order than they appear. Play bingo. When the teacher calls a word, cover it. Whoever gets 4 in a row vertically, horizontally, or any 4 corners wins.

Words: line plot, quarter, equivalent, calculate, parallel, round, angle, vertical, parallelogram, quadrilateral, square, 3D shape, 2D shape.

Write a word in each space.

Wednesday: Guess My Number

Read the riddle. Think about the clues. Discuss which answer from the right-hand column you think is correct with a classmate'?

I am a fraction that is greater than $\frac{1}{2}$.	$\frac{5}{12}$ $\frac{6}{8}$
I am less than 1.	
My numerator is not odd.	$\frac{1}{4}$ $\frac{9}{6}$
My denominator is even.	
What number am I?	

Thursday: Number Talk

Pick a number from each circle. Make an addition problem. Write the problem under the way you solved it.

Did I do it in my head?	Did I use a model?	Did I write down the numbers and solve it on paper?

A. Write four 4 digit numbers.

Pick your own numbers!

B. Write four 3 or 4 digit numbers.

Pick your own numbers!

Friday: Make Your Own Problem

Write a multiplication or division word problem. Model your thinking. Solve it.

Week 37 Teacher Notes

Monday: Pattern That!

Students have to look at the pattern and figure out what comes next. They should be ready to discuss their thinking with a math partner.

Tuesday: Vocabulary Bingo

Students put each of the words in a box in a different order than they appear. When the teacher calls a word, the students should cover it. Whoever gets 4 in a row vertically, horizontally, or any of the 4 corners, wins. The teacher should call the word, give a definition or show an illustration.

Wednesday: Convince Me!

This routine is about getting students to defend and justify their thinking. Be sure to emphasize the language of reasoning. Students should focus on proving it with numbers, words, and pictures. They should say things like:

This is true! I can prove it with….

This is the difference because….

I am going to use _____ to show my thinking.

I am going to defend my answer by _____.

Thursday: Number Talk

Students pick a number from each circle and make a subtraction problem. They should write the problem under the way they solved it. For example, ". I did 164 minus 30 and I got 134."

Friday: Word Problem Fill-in

Students fill in the word problem with their own numbers and model and solve the problem.

Week 37 Activities

Monday: Pattern That!

Make a pattern that adds 5, then subtracts 1.

Tuesday: Vocabulary Bingo

Write a word in each space.

Words: line plot, elapsed time, half past, quarter til, quarter after, hour, minute hand, hour hand, parallelogram, parallel, intersecting, trapezoid, quadrilateral, kite, rhombus, square.

Wednesday: Convince Me!

Fill in the blanks with fractions to make the sentence true.

Convince me that ____ is more than _____. Prove it!

Thursday: Number Talk

Pick a number from each circle. Make a subtraction problem. Write the problem under the way you solved it.

Did I do it in my head?	Did I use a model?	Did I write down the numbers and solve it on paper?

A. Write four 3 digit numbers.   B.

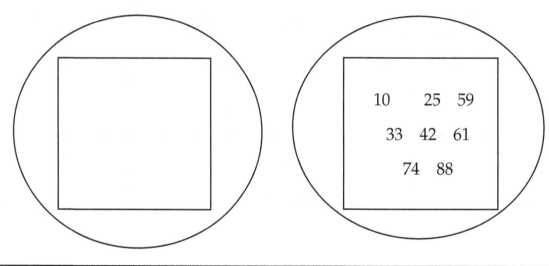

10   25   59

33   42   61

74   88

Friday: Word Problem Fill-in

The bakery has _____ boxes. There are _____ cupcakes in each box. How many cupcakes do they have altogether?

Week 38 Teacher Notes

Monday: Vocabulary Tic Tac Toe

Students will play Tic Tac Toe. They are working on discussing their strategies and finding the correct products and quotients.

Tuesday: Vocabulary Bingo

Students put each of the words in a box in a different order than they appear. When the teacher calls a word, the students should cover it. Whoever gets 4 in a row vertically, horizontally, or any of the 4 corners, wins. The teacher should call the word, give a definition or show an illustration.

Wednesday: Guess My Number

Students have to read the riddle. They should think about the clues and discuss what they think the answer is with a classmate.

Thursday: Number Talk

Students pick a number from each circle and make a subtraction problem. They should decide how they will solve it and write the problem under the way they solved it.

Friday: Word Problem Fill-in

Students fill in the word problem with their own numbers and model and solve the problem.

Monday: Vocabulary Tic Tac Toe

Do rock, paper, scissors to decide who goes first. Pick a square. Write a description or draw a picture of the answer on the side. Then, put an x or o. If your partner disagrees, look it up. If the player is correct, they go again. If wrong, they lose the turn.

3 x 3	4 x 4	5 x 5	42 ÷ 6	0 ÷ 8	24 ÷ 3
10 x 10	9 x 9	8 x 8	4 ÷ 1	45 ÷ 9	24 ÷ 2
7 x 7	6 x 6	2 x 2	15 ÷ 5	63 ÷ 7	9 ÷ 9

Tuesday: Vocabulary Bingo

Put each of the words in a box in a different order than they appear. Play bingo. When the teacher calls a word, cover it. Whoever gets 4 in a row vertically, horizontally, or any 4 corners wins.

Words: array, attribute, a.m., p.m., square units, yard, data, digit, gram, kilogram, liter, milliliter, meter, centimeter, area, perimeter.

Write a word in each space.

Wednesday: Guess My Number

Read the riddle. Think about the clues. Discuss which answer from the right-hand column you think is correct with a classmate.

I am a fraction that is less than $\frac{1}{2}$. My numerator is not odd. My denominator is even. I am equivalent to one-fourth. What number am I?	$\frac{3}{12}$ $\frac{2}{8}$ $\frac{2}{3}$ $\frac{3}{6}$

Thursday: Number Talk

Pick a number from each circle. Make a subtraction problem. Write the problem under the way you solved it.

Did I do it in my head?	Did I use a model?	Did I write down the numbers and solve it on paper?

A.

Pick your own numbers!

B.

Pick your own numbers!

Friday: Word Problem Fill-in

Fill in the blanks and solve the problem. Model your thinking.

Mary walked ___ of a mile. Kelly walked ____ of a mile. Who walked further? How do you know? Prove it.

Monday: Input/Output Table

Students fill in the missing numbers in the table based on the criteria.

Tuesday: Vocabulary Reflection

Students reflect on the vocabulary they have learned this year.

Wednesday: True or False?

Students read the expressions and decide if they are true or false. They then make their own expressions.

Thursday: Number Talk

Students pick a number from each circle and make a subtraction problem. They should decide how they will solve it and write the problem under the way they solved it. For example, "I did 170 – 50. I got 120."

Friday: Write Your Own Problem

Students have to write their own multiplication problem, solve it, and model it.

Monday: Input/Output Table

Make a function table with a rule of dividing by 2.

In	Out

Tuesday: Vocabulary Reflection

Write down 5 vocabulary words that you have learned this year. Tell your partner what they mean. Be ready to discuss them with the class.

Wednesday: True or False?

Look at the equations on the left-hand side. Decide which ones are true and which ones are false. Circle the equations that are true. On the right-hand side, write your own true or false equations. Circle the ones that are true.

True or false?	Make your own and share it out
$(2 \times 7) + (2 \times 7) = 4 \times 7$ $2 \times 7 = 8 \times 3$ $5 \times 2 = 20 \div 2$	

Thursday: Number Talk

Pick a number from each circle. Compare them. Write the problem under the way you solved it.

Did I do it in my head?	Did I use a model?	Did I write down the numbers and solve it on paper?

A.

1/2   1/4   1/5

2/6 3/4   5/5

1/3   4/3

B.

1/2   2/4   3/5

4/6 1/5   3/3

1/6   4/5

Friday: Write Your Own Problem

Write, model, and solve a word problem.

The answer is 10 marbles. Write a multiplication or division problem. Solve it.

Week 40 Teacher Notes

Monday: Input/Output Table

Students fill in the table according to the criteria.

Tuesday: Vocabulary Bingo

Students put each of the words in a box in a different order than they appear. When the teacher calls a word, the students should cover it. Whoever gets 4 in a row vertically, horizontally, or any of the 4 corners, wins. The teacher should call the word, give a definition or show an illustration.

Wednesday: Number of the Day

Students fill in the chart to represent the number.

Thursday: Number Talk

Students pick a number from each circle and make a problem. They should write the problem under the way they solved it (using any operation). For example, "I can do that in my head. I added 165 and 29. I made the problem 164 and 30 and I got 194."

Friday: Write Your Own Problem

Students write, model, and solve their own word problem.

Monday: Input/Output Table

Make a function table with a rule. Name the rule.

In	Out

Tuesday: Vocabulary Bingo

Put each of the words in a box in a different order than they appear. Play bingo. When the teacher calls a word, cover it. Whoever gets 4 in a row vertically, horizontally, or diagonally between any 4 corners wins.

Words: array, attribute, column, row, odd, even, round survey, denominator, numerator, fraction, equivalent, decompose, equal groups, array, frequency table.

Wednesday: Number of the Day

Choose your own number of the day. Fill in the boxes.

Number word form	Show addition sentences that equal your number
Write a subtraction sentence that equals your number	Add 3 numbers that equal your number

Thursday: Number Talk

Pick a number from each circle. Make a problem. Solve it using any operation. Write the problem under the way you solved it.

Did I do it in my head?	Did I use a model?	Did I write down the numbers and solve it on paper?

A. Pick your own numbers!

B. Pick your own numbers!

Friday: Write Your Own Problem

Write, model, and solve your own word problem.

Answer Key

Week 1

Monday: What Doesn't Belong?

$6 + 4 + 3$; $50 - 25$.

Tuesday: Vocabulary Match

Sum – the answer to an addition problem; addend – one of the numbers in an addition equation; centimeter – a small unit of measure; difference – the answer to a subtraction problem; hexagon – 6-sided figure.

Wednesday: Convince Me!

Answers vary: 2 possibilities – Students may count up or subtract back.

Thursday: Number Talk

Answers vary: 2 possibilities: Students might break it apart $20 + 20 + 17$ or make 29 a 30 and then add 27.

Friday: What's the Question?

Answers vary: Some possibilities are: How many are there altogether? How many more blue marbles are there than pink ones? How many red and pink marbles are there? How many fewer pink are there than blue ones?

Week 2

Monday: Magic Squares

A.

4	9	2
3	5	7
8	1	6

B.

2	9	4
7	5	3
6	1	8

Tuesday: Vocabulary Tic Tac Toe

Answers vary. For example, students could draw pictures or write definitions.

Wednesday: Number Line It!

50, 99, 182, 230, 350, 475 should be placed on number line spaced appropriately.

Thursday: Number Talk

Answers vary.

Friday: Sort That!

Join problems are A. and C.; take away problems are B. and D.

Week 3

Monday: Always, Sometimes, Never

Sometimes.

Tuesday: Vocabulary Bingo

Students discuss vocabulary; teacher calls out words by giving definitions and/or drawing examples.

Wednesday: Number of the Day

99; answers vary for addition sentences and subtraction sentences. Could be 44 + 55 and 100 − 1; 33 + 33 + 33.

Thursday: Number Strings

14, 13, 12, 11, 12, 22, 23, 24, 25.

Friday: Model That!

120

Week 4

Monday: Magic Square

8	1	6
3	5	7
4	9	2

Tuesday: It Is/It Isn't

Answers vary. For example: It is odd. It is not even. It is a 2-digit number. It is not a 1-digit number.

Wednesday: Greather Than, Less Than, in Between

Answers vary.

Thursday: Number Talk

Answers vary: 2 possibilities: count up from 29; count back from 74. Students can also make an easier problem: 74–29 can be 75–30. Answer: 45.

Friday: Picture That!

Answers vary. Possibilities: Students might tell an addition story or a multiplication story. For example: In the bakery, there were 2 rows of 3 donuts in a box. How many donuts were there altogether?

Week 5

Monday: 2 Arguments

Maria is correct.

Tuesday: Vocabulary Match

hundreds – 160; hexagon – ; thousands – 4,091; expanded form – 100 + 30 + 5; trapezoid –

Wednesday: Money Mix

Answers vary. Possibilities: 2 quarters; 1 half dollar; 5 dimes.

Thursday: Number Talk

Answers vary. Students share their thinking.

Friday: Make Your Own Problem

Answers vary. Students should discuss their models and their strategies.

Week 6

Monday: It Is/It Isn't

Answers vary. Possibilities: It is a polygon. It is a closed figure. It is a 6-sided figure. It is not a quadrilateral. It is not a parallelogram.

Tuesday: 1-Minute Essay/Quick Write

Answers vary. Students should discuss how they are closed figures. They have 3 or more sides, angles, and vertices. We name them by their attributes.

Wednesday: Find and Fix the Error

Students should be able to explain how the answer isn't reasonable. The answer is 41.

Thursday: Number Strings

29 + 4 = 33; 19 + 24 = 43; 29 + 64 = 93; 59 + 74 =133; focus should be on making the 9 a 10.

Friday: Equation Match

B. ? + 71 = 100.

Week 7

Monday: 3 Truths and a Fib

The fib is a baseball bat is about 40 yards long.

Tuesday: Vocabulary Brainstorm

Answers vary. Students can show their thinking with numbers, pictures, and words.

Wednesday: Patterns/Skip Counting

106, 104, 102, 100, 98, 96; 55, 57, 59, 61, 63, 65, 67, 69, 71; answers vary.

Thursday: Number Talk

Answers vary. Possible strategies: Count up or back. Students could also make an easier problem and change 91–54 into 97–60.

Friday: Equation Match

Problem B.

Week 8

Monday: True or False?

True.

Tuesday: Vocabulary Tic Tac Toe

Have students discuss words after their game.

Wednesday: Number Bond It!

Answers Vary. Possibilities: 23 + 33; 20 + 20 + 16; 55 + 1.

Thursday: Number Talk

Answers vary.

Friday: Model That!

Mike had 79. Together they had 156.

J | 77 |

? ↕

M | | +2 |

Week 9

Monday: Convince Me!

Answers vary. Students could use pictures, words, or numbers.

Tuesday: Vocabulary Match

Equal sign =, Less than < , minus sign –, greater than >, plus sign +.

Wednesday: Patterns/Skip Counting

Answers vary.

Thursday: Number Strings

You want students to talk about making the 9 into the nearest 10 by adding 1 to each number.

Friday: Picture That!

Answers vary. For example: A carton had 87 oranges. What is a good estimate?

Week 10

Monday: Reasoning Matrices

Jenny – chocolate, Jamal – pecan, Miguel – strawberry, Kelly – lemon, Maria – cherry, Grace – pumpkin.

Tuesday: Vocabulary Tic Tac Toe

Answers vary.

Wednesday: Number of the Day

247

Word form Two hundred and forty–seven	10 more 257	10 less 237
Expanded form 200 + 40 + 7	_____ + _____ = 247 Answers vary	_____ – _____ = 247 Answers vary
Base ten sketch 	How many more to 500? 253	Odd or even? odd
100 more 347	100 less 147	247 – _____ = _____ Answers vary

Thursday: Number Talk

Answers vary. Students can talk about making the 49 into a 50 and the 55 into a 54. They could also add the tens and then the ones.

Friday: Write a Problem

Answers vary. For example: Grandma made 25 chocolate cupcakes and 35 strawberry ones. How many did she make altogether?

Week 11

Monday: Venn Diagram

Answers vary: i.e. by

    Numbers less than 20: 1, 2, 3, 4, 5
    Numbers greater than 20: 21, 22, 23, 24, 25
    Even numbers: 2, 22, 24

Tuesday: Vocabulary Bingo

Answers vary.

Wednesday: Why Is It Not?

A. It is not 20 because 20+ 6 = 26. B. A circle is not a polygon. It has no straight sides, angles, or vertices.

Thursday: Number Talk

Answers vary. Students can count up; count back; make an easier problem like 100 – 78 take away 80 and then add 2 back.

Friday: What's the Question?

Answers vary. For example: Which cookie did they have the most of? How many cookies did they have altogether?

Week 12

Monday: Legs and Feet

A. 6 legs. All other answers vary: B. 2 cows and 1 chicken or 3 chickens and 1 cow; C. 2 cows and 2 chickens; 1 cow and 4 chickens, etc.; D. 2 cows and 3 chickens; 3 cows and 1 chicken, etc.

Tuesday: Vocabulary Brainstorm

Answers vary. For example, part of a whole; numerator; denominator.

Wednesday: 3 Truths and a Fib

90 can be 90 fives is a fib.

Thursday: Number Talk

Students can talk about adding up or subtracting back.

Friday: Word Problem Sort

B. We are looking for the smaller part.

Week 13

Monday: What Doesn't Belong?

A. difference.

B. 90 – 50.

Tuesday: Frayer Model

Answers vary. Definition: Repeated addition; example 2 x 3; non-example division; (picture could be an array or equal groups).

Wednesday: Round That!

Answers vary: A. is any number from 45 to 54. B. is any number from 650 to 749.

Thursday: Number Talk

Answers vary: Students could break apart the 5 or the 7 in different ways.

Friday: What's the Question?

Answers vary. For example: How many red marbles are there? How many blue marbles are there? How many marbles are there altogether?

Week 14

Monday: Always, Sometimes, Never

A. Sometimes – when you subtract zero the number stays the same.

B. Sometimes – if you halve 14 you get 7.

Tuesday: Frayer Model

Answers vary. Definition: partitioning or sharing; example $\frac{20}{2}$; non-example multiplication; picture (students might draw an array or an equal group being divided).

Wednesday: Guess My Number

A. 75.

B. 86.

Thursday: Number Talk

Answers vary.

Friday: Picture That!

Answers vary. For example: Sue got a box of cookies. They were in a 3 by 4 array. How many cookies did she get? (Models vary – number line, array, tape diagram.)

Week 15

Monday: It Is/It Isn't

Answers vary: It is sharing or partitioning. It is not multiplication. It is not repeated addition. It is repeated subtraction.

Tuesday: Vocabulary Fill-in

A. product.

B. multiplication.

C. division.

D. array.

E. quotient.

Wednesday: Venn Diagram

Answers vary: 2 digit: 24, 10, 12, 56, 59; 3 digit: 300, 301, 303, 304; Both: 24, 10, 300, 302.

Thursday: Number Talk

Answers vary. For example, students might talk about what happens when you divide by 2 or halve a number.

Friday: What's the Question?

Answers vary. For example: How much farther did they drive on Tuesday than on Monday? How far did they drive altogether?

Week 16

Monday: What Doesn't Belong?

$\frac{10}{10}$; (2 x 2 x 7)

Tuesday: 1-Minute Essay/Quick Write

Answers vary. Students should discuss equal groups, arrays, repeated addition, etc.

Wednesday: Fraction of the Day

word form one–fourth	rectangle model
circle model	draw a line and cut it into 4 equal parts

Thursday: Number Talk

Answers vary.

Friday: Word Problem Sort

A. is the division problem. The answer is 4. B. is a 2-step problem with multiplication as one of the steps. The answer is 22.

Week 17

Monday: Input/Output Table

In	Out
2	10
3	15
4	20
5	25
6	30
7	35

In	Out
14	7
10	5
16	8
8	4
6	3
4	2

Answers vary.

In	Out

Tuesday: Vocabulary Tic Tac Toe

Answers vary.

Wednesday: What Doesn't Belong?

A. 42 doesn't round to 50.

B. 94 doesn't round to 100.

Thursday: Number Strings

Answers vary. For example, students should talk about how when multiplying by 2 the number is doubled.

Friday: Word Problem Fill-in

Answers vary.

Week 18

Monday: True or False?

1. True; 2. False; 3. Answers vary.

Tuesday: What Doesn't Belong?

Product is not a word directly related to division; ml is not a measurement of length.

Wednesday: Guess My Number

A. 56; B. 18.

Thursday: Number Talk

Answers vary. Students could take apart 7 in a variety of ways.

Friday: Picture That!

Answers vary. For example: The farmer had 5 boxes of strawberries. There were about 18 in each box. About how many strawberries did she have?

Week 19

Monday: Break It up!

$$3 \times 7$$

Sketch it!	Break it apart!
	Answers vary: Example

$$3 \times 7 = (3 \times 3) + (3 \times 4)$$

Tuesday: 1-Minute Essay/Quick Write

Answers vary. Students should talk about partitioning and/or sharing. They should use words such as quotient, divisor, and dividend. They should draw pictures of equal groups or arrays.

Wednesday: How Many More to

Start at 50 … How many more to 100? **50**

Start at 78 … How many more to 100? **22**

Start at 150 … How many more to 200? **50**

Start at 275 … How many more to 500? **225**

Start at 300 … How many more to 1,000? **700**

Thursday: Number Talk

Answers vary.

Friday: What's the Story?

Answers vary. For example: Tom had 6 boxes with 3 marbles in each box. How many marbles did he have altogether?

Week 20

Monday: True or False?

	True or False?
$5 + 10 = 3 \times 5$	True
$\dfrac{16}{8} = 2 \times 8$	False
$34 + 16 = 100 - 50$	True
$2 \times 7 = 70 - 56$	True
Make your own!	Answers vary

Tuesday: Vocabulary Brainstorm

Answers vary. Students should write about area. They should talk about multiplying the sides. They should talk about the space covered.

Wednesday: Find and Fix the Error

Answers vary. Students might talk about how he didn't regroup. They might also show different strategies to solve this problem such as counting up or adding 1 to each number (compensation).

Thursday: Number Talk

Students should discuss different strategies such as counting up or adjusting it to a ten by adding 2 to each number (compensation).

Friday: What's the Story?

Answers vary. For example: Marta had 20 rings. She put 5 in each box. How many boxes did she use?

Week 21

Monday: Alike and Different

Answers vary. For example, students might talk about how they are both quadrilaterals but they are not both parallelograms.

Tuesday: Vocabulary Bingo

Answers vary.

Wednesday: Number Bond It!

Answers vary. For example, 500 ml and 500 ml or 200 ml and 800 ml. It could also be 250 ml, 250 ml and 500 ml.

Thursday: Number Talk

Answers vary.

Friday: What's the Story?

Answers vary. For example: Dan had 6 cookies. He divided them into 2 bags. How many cookies are in each bag?

Week 22

Monday: Elapsed Time

Answers vary.

Tuesday: Frayer Model

Answers vary.

Definition: Estimating to a near number.
Examples: 57 rounds to 60.
Real life situation: Estimating cookies in a jar.
Non-examples: Counting.

Wednesday: Fraction of the Day

$$\frac{1}{2}$$

Word form half	Picture form
Plot it on the number line	Is it greater or less than $\frac{1}{4}$? How do you know? It is greater than $\frac{1}{4}$ because $\frac{1}{2}$ equals $\frac{2}{4}$.

Thursday: Number Talk

Answers vary.

Friday: What's the Story?

Answers vary. Students could talk about measuring the length of beetles, etc.

Week 23

Monday: Missing Number

A. Lucy.
B. 4.
C. 10.
D. 7.

Tuesday: Frayer Model

Answers vary.

For example:
Definition: the space an object covers.
Example: a picture of a rug.
Real life example: the area of a rug.
Non-example: the perimeter.

Wednesday: What's Missing?

A. 7, 14, 21, 28, 35, 42, 49, 56, 63.
B. 8000, 4000, 2000, 1,000, 500, 250, 125.
C. Answers vary.

Thursday: Number Talk

Answers vary.

Friday: Model That!

Part 1

10 animals	
5 turtles	? fish

$5 + 5 = 10$

Part 2

5 turtles	5 fish	7 more fish

$5 + 7 = 12$

$12 + 5 = 17$

Week 24

Monday: Input/Output Table

Answers vary. For example:

Input	Output
1	7
2	14
3	21
4	28

Tuesday: 1-Minute Essay/Quick Write

Answers vary. Students can write about fractions, numerators, denominators, parts/wholes, and they could draw pictures and write fractions.

Wednesday: Round That!

Answers vary. For example, 799, 801, and vary from 750–799.

Thursday: Number Talk

Answers vary. $\frac{1}{2} < \frac{3}{3}$; $\frac{3}{4} > \frac{1}{2}$; $\frac{2}{3} = \frac{4}{6}$.

Friday: Model That!

60 came; 100 insects altogether.

Week 25

Monday: What Doesn't Belong?

A. 16 – 9.

B. (3 x 3) + (3 x 3).

Tuesday: Vocabulary Tic Tac Toe

Answers vary.

Wednesday: Fraction of the Day

$$\frac{3}{3}$$

Word form three-thirds	Picture form 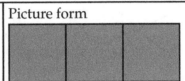
Plot it on the number line 	Is it greater or less than $\frac{6}{6}$? How do you know? It is equivalent.

Thursday: Number Talk

$$\begin{array}{r} 758 \\ -\ 552 \\ \hline 206 \end{array}$$

Friday: Model That!

25 ft.

5	5	5	5	5

$25 \div 5 = 5$

Week 26

Monday: Number Line It!

$$\frac{1}{8} \qquad \frac{3}{8} \qquad \frac{1}{2} \qquad\qquad \frac{3}{4} \qquad\qquad \frac{4}{4}$$

Tuesday: Vocabulary Match

equivalent — the part that names the pieces of the whole that we are considering

quotient — to break apart

denominator — the same as

numerator — the answer to a division problem

decompose — names the number of parts in the whole

Wednesday: Fraction of the Day

$$\frac{5}{4}$$

Word form: Five-fourths	Draw a model

Plot it on the number line:

$$\frac{4}{4} \qquad \frac{5}{4}$$

Thursday: Find and Fix the Error

$$175$$
$$\underline{+\,237}$$
$$412$$

Friday: What's the Story?

Answers vary. For example: Sue had 5 boxes. She put 2 rings in a box. How many rings did she have altogether?

Week 27

Monday: Always, Sometimes, Never

True.

Tuesday: Frayer Model

Definition	Examples
A whole divided into 4 parts	A fourth of a pie
Give a picture example	Non-example thirds

Wednesday: Patterns/Skip Counting

1. 1, 600, 800, 400, 200, 100, 50, 25.

2. 2, 4, 8, 16, 32, 64, 128, 256.

3. Make your own: Answers vary.

Thursday: Number Talk

Answers vary.

Friday: Equation Match

Problem B.

Week 28

Monday: Why Is It Not?

Answers vary: A. For example, it is not 550 because that is more than 300 and both sides have to be the same; B. It is not 30 because 3 x 30 is 90 which is more than 10.

Tuesday: It Is/It Isn't

Answers vary. 789 is not even. 789 is not a 2-digit number.

Wednesday: Number of the Day

5, 109

Word form Five thousand, one hundred and nine	10 more 5,119	10 less 5,099
Expanded form 5,000 + 100 + 9	_____ + _____ = 5,109 Answers vary	_____ – _____ = 5,109 Answers vary
100 more 5,209	How many more to 10,000? 4,891	Odd or even Odd
1,000 more 6,109	100 less 5,009	5,109 – _____ = _____ Answers vary

Thursday: Number Talk

Answers vary.

Friday: What's the Story?

Answers vary. The bakery had 210 cupcakes. They had 10 more cookies than cupcakes. How many cookies do they have? 220 cookies.

Week 29

Monday: Reasoning about Numbers

Answers vary: A. 899 + 99; B. 2099 − 1090.

Tuesday: Vocabulary Fill-in

The answer to an addition problem is called the sum.

The answer to a subtraction problem is called the difference.

A fraction is a part of a number.

Wednesday: Guess My Number

106

Thursday: Number Talk

Students should count up 2 or count back 2.

Friday: Word Problem Sort

B. It is looking for the smaller part.

Week 30

Monday: 2 Arguments

Maria. Explanations vary.

Tuesday: Vocabulary Bingo

Answers vary.

Wednesday: Number Line It!

```
←——————————————————————————→
   5      250      499      750      900     1,000
```

Thursday: Number Talk

Answers vary.

Friday: What's the Question?

Answers vary. For example, how far did they travel altogether?

Week 31

Monday: True or False?

False/True/False/True.

Tuesday: Vocabulary Brainstorm

Answers vary.

Wednesday: 3 Truths and a Fib

110 tens.

Thursday: Number Talk

Answers vary. For example $50 \div 5$ or $20 \div 2$.

Friday: Model That!

They ate the same amount.

Week 32

Monday: Reasoning about Numbers

Answers vary. For example, 3 by 8; 4 by 6; or 12 by 2.

Tuesday: Vocabulary Bingo

Answers vary.

Wednesday: Greater Than, Less Than, in Between

Answers vary.

Thursday: Number Talk

Answers vary.

Friday: What's the Question?

Answers vary but should represent 79 cents.

Week 33

Monday: Reasoning about Numbers

Students should be able to say that the size of the candy bar matters. Depending on the size of the whole, either one of the students could be correct.

Tuesday: What Doesn't Belong?

A. hexagon.

B. oval.

Wednesday: What Doesn't Belong?

A. 1 hundred tens and 5 ones.

B. 150 + 20.

Thursday: Number Talk

Answers vary. For example: 100–22.

Friday: What's the Story?

Answers vary. For example: There were several beetles in the zoo. How many were longer than 2 inches?

Week 34

Monday: Convince Me!

Answers vary.

Tuesday: Vocabulary Brainstorm

Answers vary. Students should discuss how equivalent fractions are the same amount but cut up into different sizes. They could give examples with numbers and pictures.

Wednesday: Find and Fix the Error

Students should discuss how he didn't add correctly and then different strategies to do it correctly. For example, they could make 79 into 80 and the 108 into 107 and add that to get 187.

Thursday: Number Talk

Answers vary.

Friday: What's the Question?

Answers vary. How many gold rings do they have? How many silver rings do they have? How many rings do they have altogether?

Week 35

Monday: 3 Truths and a Fib

Kilometers measures width is a fib.

Tuesday: Vocabulary Tic Tac Toe

Answers vary.

Wednesday: Number Bond It!

Answers vary. For example: 20 + 30 + 24 or 36 + 38.

Thursday: Number Talk

Answers vary.

Friday: Pattern That!

Part A. Not here.

Part B. Answers vary.

Week 36

Monday: True or False?

False.

Tuesday: Vocabulary Bingo

Answers vary.

Wednesday: Guess My Number.

$\dfrac{6}{8}$

Thursday: Number Talk

Answers vary.

Friday: Make Your Own Problem

Answers vary.

Week 37

Monday: Pattern That!

Answers vary. For example: 7, 12, 11, 16, 15, 20.

Tuesday: Vocabulary Bingo

Answers vary.

Wednesday: Convince Me!

Answers vary.

Thursday: Number Talk

Answers vary.

Friday: Word Problem Fill-in

Answers vary.

Week 38

Monday: Vocabulary Tic Tac Toe

3 × 3 9	4 × 4 16	5 × 5 25
10 × 10 100	9 × 9 81	8 × 8 64
7 × 7 49	6 × 6 36	2 × 2 4

42 ÷ 6 7	0 ÷ 8 0	24 ÷ 3 8
4 ÷ 1 4	45 ÷ 9 5	24 ÷ 2 12
15 ÷ 5 3	63 ÷ 7 9	9 ÷ 9 1

Tuesday: Vocabulary Bingo

Answers vary.

Wednesday: Guess My Number.

$\frac{2}{8}$

Thursday: Number Talk

Answers vary. For example 20 + 24 + 75 + 75.

Friday: Word Problem Fill-in

Answers vary.

Week 39

Monday: Input/Output Table

Answers vary.

Tuesday: Vocabulary Reflection

Answers vary.

Wednesday: True or False?

True; False; True.

Thursday: Number Talk

Answers vary. $\dfrac{1}{2} < \dfrac{3}{3}$; $\dfrac{3}{4} > \dfrac{1}{2}$; $\dfrac{2}{3} = \dfrac{4}{6}$.

Friday: Write Your Own Problem

Answers vary.

Week 40

Monday – Friday: Answers vary.

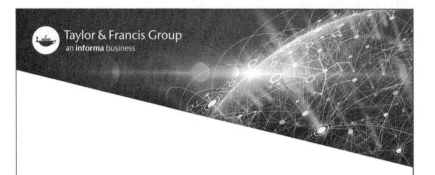

For Product Safety Concerns and Information please contact our EU
representative GPSR@taylorandfrancis.com Taylor & Francis Verlag GmbH,
Kaufingerstraße 24, 80331 München, Germany

Printed and bound by CPI Group (UK) Ltd, Croydon, CR0 4YY
08/06/2025
01896981-0003